A FESTIVAL OF
Violin & Fiddle Styles
FOR CELLO

BY JULIE LYONN LIEBERMAN

To access audio and video, visit:
www.halleonard.com/mylibrary

Enter Code
6080-7698-1815-4660

ISBN 978-1-5400-5778-5

Visit Hal Leonard Online at
www.halleonard.com

Contact us:
Hal Leonard
7777 West Bluemound Road
Milwaukee, WI 53213
Email: info@halleonard.com

In Europe, contact:
Hal Leonard Europe Limited
42 Wigmore Street
Marylebone, London, W1U 2RN
Email: info@halleonardeurope.com

In Australia, contact:
Hal Leonard Australia Pty. Ltd.
4 Lentara Court
Cheltenham, Victoria, 3192 Australia
Email: info@halleonard.com.au

Photo Credits:
Julie Lyonn Lieberman, photo by Leonard V. Cascia (p.3)
Tom Morley, photo by August Bruce (p.15)
Electric Violin Shop array of instruments, photo by Matt Bell (p.35)
Tanya Kalmanovitch, photo by Bethany Bandera (p.39)
Dave Reiner, photo by Joni Lohr (p.40)
Don and Cindy Roy, photo by Molly Haley (p.50)
Jason Anick, photo by Sasha Israel (p.53)
Chris Haigh, photo by Mike Samson (p.90)
Andrea Hoag, photo by Michael G. Stewart (p.114)

Cover Photos:
Spur violin, NS NXT electric violin and Paul Davies acoustic

Section Covers designed by Loren Moss Meyer:
How to Play the World—Spur Violin by Paul Davies
American Roots Styles—Acoustic violin by Paul Davies
American Popular Styles—NS NXT solid-body violin by Ned Steinberger
Latin Styles—Violin art by Len Cascia

Notation Consultants:
David Finch, Dawn Gaylord, and Madeline Herdeman

Design, page layout, notation, video tutorials and backing tracks by Julie Lyonn Lieberman

ACKNOWLEDGMENTS

It takes more than a village to write a book like this one. I consider myself deeply fortunate to be in the company of a group of special souls dedicated to preserving tradition as well as lending their creativity to propel bowed strings into the 21st century. I am also extremely grateful to Paul Davies for my Spur violin, pictured on page 9 as well as to Gary Byers and Ned Steinberger for my NS NXT violin, pictured on page 55.

Special thanks to...

Jay Ungar for writing the preface; Loren Moss Meyer for her design wizardry and eagle eyes, Matt Wolf for overseeing the project, Max Fischer for translating my ideas into a book cover, and my long-time liaison at Hal Leonard, Jeff Schroedl, to whom I am eternally grateful.

Deep appreciation for the endorsement quotes on the back cover:

Darol Anger, Bruce Molsky, Mark Wood, and Rachel Barton Pine.

Many thanks to my colleagues for sharing their expertise:

Tanya Kalmanovitch, Abby Newton, Aly Bain, Andrea Beaton, Beth Bahia Cohen, Bruce Molsky, Chris Haigh, Darol Anger, Dave Reiner, Calvin Vollrath, Joe Deninzon, Mark Wood, Jason Anick, Jeremy Cohen, Katie Glassman, Andrea Hoag, Melinda Crawford, Don Roy, Paul Anastasio, Roby Lakatos, Tom Morley, Vicki Richards, Yale Strom, Sam Bardfeld, and David Finch.

Note: Quotes from Howard Armstrong, Dr. Billy Taylor and Alan Jabbour were excerpted from 1989 interviews for my National Public Radio series, *The Talking Violin*.

Special thanks to David Finch, Dawn Gaylord, and Madeline Herdeman for providing feedback on the violin, viola, and cello clef transpositions.

CONTENTS

PREFACE BY JAY UNGAR

Many fiddlers are deeply focused on one style of music, but I've always been drawn to multiple musical styles. I guess that made me more of a "jack of all styles" kind of fiddler, but eventually I created my own musical niche by building my style based on the music that touched me most deeply. And of course, my family and the environment I grew up in were big influences.

My dad, who grew up on a dairy farm in Hungary, sang mournful Hungarian folk songs on long drives when I was a kid. He was a very emotional singer and I'm sure this had an effect on me and my music. My mom told me that I was drawn to music from birth. Growing up in a rough neighborhood in the South Bronx, music was my safe place, my place of refuge. I begged for music lessons when I was six and my parents finally let me start when I was seven. My mom took me to a local music teacher who offered a variety of instruments. I don't know why I chose the violin, but that choice clearly shaped the course of my life.

My violin lessons were strictly classical, but I also loved to pick up tunes by ear from records, movies, radio and TV—whatever I heard that caught my fancy. I loved playing by ear and the freedom and creativity that it provided. The classical composers whose music I was most drawn to—though I didn't understand why at the time—were Bartok, Tchaikovsky and Copland, who'd woven folk tunes, hymns, and dance rhythms into their compositions. I also loved the spontaneous, playful flow in Bach's and Mozart's compositions, a quality reminiscent of improvisation.

Several experiences in my childhood greatly influenced the path of my life and music. As a student at the High School of Music and Art in New York City, I encountered two sides of a significant divide. The conductor of the senior orchestra created a highly competitive environment in which members of the violin section were forced to compete with one another—sometimes weekly—for their positions in the section. Conversely, the conductor of the senior chamber orchestra created a collaborative environment, where we all worked together to achieve the fullest potential of each piece of music. The feeling of having accomplished something beautiful together was a wonderful gift. I didn't realize it at the time, but this was life-changing for me.

I had a friend in high school who played the banjo and introduced me to bluegrass and old-time music. I had always felt out of place in the City and was instantly drawn to this music because of its rural roots. At the time I mistakenly thought that all fiddle music came from the southern mountains. I eventually learned that every region of North America has a fiddle style of its own, even my native New York State. I discovered that one of the primary functions of fiddle music worldwide is to bring people together at dances and celebrations. I love that!

As a young fiddler trying to earn a living, I worked with musicians who could play many styles of music, so we could say yes to virtually any and every gig that came in—from apple season at the local cider mill where we played songs and fiddle tunes related to farming and harvest season, to jazz standards, waltzes and a variety of ethnic styles for upscale weddings. During that stretch in my life when I sometimes played two or three weddings in a weekend, I realized that a wedding musician can help create a real sense of community and recognition when he or she includes the members of both families by playing music that's meaningful to them. This might mean performing anything from Irish, Scottish, Latin,

Jewish, or Greek music to blues, jazz and contemporary popular songs. How gratifying and what fun!

My wife Molly Mason and I have become known for playing historic American music, mainly through our many collaborations with documentary filmmaker Ken Burns. And over the decades, we've immersed ourselves in regional American fiddle styles at our Ashokan Music & Dance Camps. Since there are no recordings of 18th and scant few of 19th century music, we don't pretend to play it with strict authenticity. Instead we let the music guide us as we try to play with the feeling and enthusiasm it might have enjoyed in the day.

Learning to play a traditional fiddle style is like learning a language. Folks who've grown up in a musical tradition have heard it from birth. To play creatively within a tradition, you first need to master the language and the accent. So, lots of listening is needed to understand and begin to emulate the rhythmic, melodic and harmonic subtleties of any genre. Then the fun can really begin!

Ultimately, my musical odyssey has been about striking a balance between helping preserve musical traditions of the past and humbly adding to them in my own way. If I've added something of value, it might stick. If not, no worries, it will be quickly forgotten. In either case I've had a ton of fun along the way. I'm thrilled to see so many fine young fiddlers who love the old tunes and are writing new tunes of their own. My dear friend and mentor, Cajun fiddler Dewey Balfa, used to say that a musical tradition is like a tree. "You have to water the roots to keep the tree alive, but you can't cut off the branches every time it tries to grow."

A NOTE FROM JULIE

I am—and have always been—in love with the musical imagination of the world. Primarily a multi-genre improviser and composer, my personal intent has not been focused on mastering one style above all others. Think of me like a honeybee who has traveled flower-to-flower, collecting and combining nectar from a variety of species. And now I'm here to share the honey. Each style I've pursued has improved my listening skills, dexterity on the instrument, and ability to understand the threads that connect, as well as differentiate how each culture in the world hears.

In the past, classically trained players didn't understand the value of learning home-bred string styles, and fiddlers tended to stick with one style. Thankfully, this has changed incrementally over the years. *A Festival of Violin and Fiddle Styles* will support your exploration into incredibly diverse musical topographies, and hopefully stimulate an appreciation and respect for the jewels offered by each.

It still tickles me to think back to my earliest venture into roots styles. When I was young, my family was deeply involved in folk music. We attended concerts on a regular basis and members of my family helped create The Folk Music Society of Northern New Jersey. But my private instruction was classical. In those days, the Internet did not yet exist. It took me a long time to find a book with fiddle tunes. I sent in my $9.95—a lot of money for me, requiring several babysitting jobs to raise it—and then I waited five weeks for it to arrive. Finally, that slim book, which I still own, arrived in the mail. I eagerly pulled it out of its mailing envelope, excitedly placed it on my music stand, and played through every single tune. Then, I threw the book on the floor in utter disgust as I turned to my cat, Tawney, and said, "This is just a book full of short classical tunes."

In those days, it was expected the player already knew how to stylize the tunes they saw on the printed page, so each book—whether old-time or Irish—offered a collection of melodies without much instruction as to how to play them correctly. And we didn't have instructional videos back then. It wasn't until my cousins began to book the U.S. tours for The Boys of the Lough, a renowned Irish group, that I had the opportunity to hang out with Aly Bain, Dave Richardson, Cathal McConnell, and Robin Morton, and learn by ear while watching them rehearse and perform up close. I still have pages of tunes Dave took the time to write out for me because my ears weren't yet strong enough to pick up the melodies by ear.

For Classically Trained String Teachers

More and more string teachers are interested in teaching roots styles in their private studio or classroom, but many teachers don't know how to play or teach those styles or may only specialize in one. Their students ultimately end up playing melodies from various genres without distinction. If this situation applies to you, this resource will provide the tools you'll need to help your students recognize, master, and enjoy the garden of musical possibilities.

It has always been my belief that string students should be exposed to the styles created on their home soil. The argument that only classical training can provide high levels of musicianship no longer holds. Every style shares the same objectives: good intonation, tone, coordination and musicianship. The only way you, as a teacher, can learn about and master the unique challenges offered by each style, is to roll up your sleeves and explore the bountiful stream of bowed string music. So...welcome!

HOW
TO PLAY
THE WORLD

~ Essential Techniques

~ How to Capture the Style

~ Four Ways to Learn a Melody

~ Are Chords Worth Learning?

~ The Art of Accompaniment

~ How to Generate Variations

ESSENTIAL TECHNIQUES

Even within classical repertoire, techniques needed to play Bartok are radically different from the techniques needed to play Bach, and each style in the world calls for different bowing and fingering techniques. Structures can vary in length, and there are differing concepts about what type of scale to use, and whether or not its notes remain consistent throughout the tune. The groove, something that's nearly impossible to convey through notation, is maintained by the rhythm instruments used by the culture, but the string player's bow arm must learn how to capture its sound and feel.

American string players are responsible for the creation of at least six distinct styles: Appalachian, blues, Cajun, bluegrass, Franco-American, and Western Swing. American styles like rock, swing, as well as jazz—all outgrowths of the blues—require yet another set of listening, playing and cognitive techniques. Popular string-centric genres found throughout the world include Irish, Scottish, Klezmer, Scandinavian (in particular but not limited to Swedish and Norwegian), Romany (Gypsy), Tango, Gypsy Jazz, Cape Breton, Québécois (Keh-beh-kwah), Afro-Cuban, East Indian, Shetland Island, and Flamenco, to name a few. These styles add to the number of distinctly unique musical fingerprints available to string players. There are a number of styles that are equally wonderful to explore even though they aren't specifically string-centric, including Bollywood, Cape Verde, and Reggae. There are also musical styles that include different bowed string instruments, like the African *gonje* (gah-n-gee) or the Chinese *erhu* (arr-hoo).

If you're wondering why it's worth the effort to master more than one style, or whether or not it's even possible, think of this book as a resource ready to serve you as your musical appetite shifts or expands. The skill set you've worked hard to build to date will not be compromised or lost; it will be magnified. And sometimes, trying something new might not appeal to you right away. It may be an acquired taste that requires time to develop.

The tunes in this book will enable you to develop new techniques and help direct your listening skills along byways you may not have already explored. *A Festival of Violin and Fiddle Styles* will provide you with a jam-packed travelogue through the musical ingenuity of many different cultures. Each style includes a tune, and most have been packaged with left- and right-hand tips, technical and musical exercises designed to help you capture the style, as well as a glimpse into its place of origin. If you aren't comfortable reading music, no worries. You can use the audio examples to learn each tune by ear and then jam with the backing tracks on the Hal Leonard *MyLibrary* website: *www.halleonard.com/mylibrary* .

HOW TO CAPTURE THE STYLE

Bowed string players invest an enormous amount of attention into the trajectory the pitches follow and the rhythmic units that shape and support those pitches. All the while, we hone intonation for every pitch. The nature of playing a bowed string instrument tends to funnel our attention into the melody line, with the expectation that the bow arm will follow along. However, almost all the styles offered in this book were originally crafted to accompany dance, so the ability to identify and echo each style will require listening for and duplicating a wider range of attributes, in particular, the groove. And, of course, each style has innovated its own set of techniques.

Here are some questions you can ask yourself while listening to a new style. These questions will support you as you pursue mastering the unique characteristics of each tune.

THE LEFT HAND

Vibrato

Does this style employ vibrato? If so, what kind? Is it slow or fast, wide or narrow? Does the sound require full, half, or close to zero pressure? Is it applied throughout, or only used to emphasize certain notes within each phrase? Where, within the measure or phrase, does the style in question include vibrato?

Slides

Are slides featured within the style? If so, are the slides short or long, fast or slow? Are they varied or the same?

Ornamentation

Does this style utilize ornamentation? If so, what kind? Which notes within the phrase are ornamented? Which notes are articulated without ornamentation? Are the ornaments subtle or featured? What does the bow do when a note is ornamented? Does it accentuate the ornament, the melody note, both, or neither?

The Right Hand

Inflections

Are all the notes played evenly throughout, or does the bow accentuate certain pitches? Subtler yet, does the bow place an accent at the inception of the pitch, in the middle, or toward the end? Is the accent understated or hard-hitting? If more than one, where do the accents tend to occur within the overall phrase?

 INFLECTIONS

Bow Speed

Are there key moments within each phrase when the motion of the bow speeds up or slows down? Is a change in speed related to a change in bow pressure? What effect is achieved, and where in the measure or phrase does it occur?

 BOW SPEED

Slurs

Slurs will influence the way a tune dances over the walking beat, particularly when the bowing pattern is repetitive. Does the style apply a slur or slurs at important spots within the tune? If so, where within the measure? Or is it random?

 SLURS

Geography

Does the style call for a particular bow stroke length? A set location on the bow? A preference for bow direction? If so, where within the phrase?

 BOW GEOGRAPHY

The "fiddle" and the "violin" are really the same instrument. Each name implies the style of music played by the musician. A few "fiddlers" like to flatten their bridges a little to make it easier to play double stops.

GENERAL CHARACTERISTICS

Meter

Does the style prefer a particular meter? For instance, Irish tunes tend to be played in 4/4 (reels), 6/8 (jigs) and 9/8 (slip jigs).

Rhythmic Content

Are specific rhythmic values favored? If so, which ones? Eighths? Dotted eighths? Triplets? Sixteenths? Syncopation? Anticipation of the next beat?

Rhythmic Emphasis

If the tune is in 4/4 time, does the style favor emphasis on the first and third beats of the measure, or on the second and fourth beats?

IMPORTANT CONSIDERATIONS

Music Notation versus "The Real Thang"

For those of you who tend to learn repertoire by reading music, it's important to remember the difference between how to interpret notation for material derived from Western canon, versus roots styles. For instance, while eighth notes are a universal currency and are notated the same way for all styles, they are interpreted differently for swing music versus Latin or Celtic. Another example is the bowed treble. This Irish rhythm, used within many Irish tunes, is notated like a triplet, but played closer to two sixteenths followed by an eighth note.

Therefore, it is essential to listen to recorded examples or videos of each tune you wish to learn. Or, if you can't find a recording for the specific tune, listen to other tunes in that style.

Aural Learners

For just about every roots music style, learning a tune by ear has been favored over notation for centuries. There are advantages and shortfalls to ears versus eyes. The reading musician is able to see the entire tune at once, and in an instant, detect the phrases that repeat, where the melody is mirrored an octave lower or higher, the number of measures, the form, and many other details that aren't immediately apparent when learning by ear, which is more a linear process.

The default for many aural learners is to master the tune a note or phrase at a time, starting at the beginning and moving little by little to the end. If you're an aural learner, you can counterbalance this approach by paying attention to the characteristics outlined throughout this introductory section.

Technical Habits from Classical Training

Habits are extremely useful. They can provide the mental space for you to turn your attention to other, more immediate issues while playing. If you started out as a classically-trained player, you have likely developed some useful technical habits for Western canon, but they could be so deeply ingrained you might not notice them. Many of these physical moves will not serve you well when attempting to play authentically in other styles.

Primarily, the habits that will require re-training include over-bowing, symmetrical pressure, legato-vibrato and "march, march, march." Most of these issues—except vibrato—pertain to the bow hand. Don't worry, you won't spoil or lose anything you've already achieved; on the contrary, you'll develop more detailed listening skills as well as a keener mind-to-body relationship, to widen your technical vocabulary.

Over-bowing: Classically-trained players are generally taught to use long bows to get a full sound. This prepares them to play in an orchestra or as a soloist, since amplification isn't utilized in either case. Each genre has its own guidelines when it comes to how much bow length to use. In the case of Western canon, techniques like spiccato, staccato, martelé, tremolo, or ricochet call for short bow-strokes, but those techniques contribute to our next issue on the list.

Symmetrical bow motion: Short and long bows for Western canon often require an attack at initiation followed by symmetrical pressure throughout. Most other genres will challenge you to make sensitive distinctions in pressure. Sometimes, certain notes will require subtle swells halfway, three-quarters of the way, or even toward the end of the note. These swells are far more subtle than the type of accent required for classical literature. And few of these styles will call for attacks on the beginning of the note.

Legato vibrato: Training and gravity invite players to leave the bow on the string unless notated to the contrary. Those ingrained habits we've been discussing, and the moment the bow sweeps up and down. The left hand, like a racehorse at the gate when the gun goes off, will begin its signature rolling motion. But most roots styles don't call for vibrato, and if they do, it's more like a seasoning rather than an ongoing effect. For instance, a slow, wide vibrato can be more appropriate for the blues; whereas in rock, we often use a wide, fast and extremely light motion that's more like ice-skating than rolling. Listen to examples from important players in each style for guidance.

March, march, march: Throughout the world, the music of many cultures was originally conceived as a practice integral to community for spiritual worship or to accompany dance. The art of performance is fairly recent to cultures worldwide. Western canon emphasizes the walking beat and the first and third beats of the measure. While Western culture leaned toward a more of a processional type of foot motion, or waltzes, the majority of footwork for dances worldwide emphasized lifting the feet off the ground, thus the emphasis on beats two and four.

The marching beat leans toward a symmetrical emphasis, so learning how to lighten the motion of the bow so it constantly modulates pressure into the string will take some practice. But eventually, your bow arm will bob, weave, and dance.

When I approach a new style, I'm always comparing and contrasting what I hear in a genre with what I already know and play. For example, slurs and double stops: in Irish music the style is mostly clean, single-note playing as contrasted with plenty of open-string drones in old-time or the use of clever double-stop intervals in bluegrass. I notice whether I hear a lot of single notes or groups  *of two, three, or more notes in a slur, interspersed between single bows. In bowing, Irish music requires a light, almost-Baroque touch often in the upper third of the bow, whereas old-time players like to use the middle of the bow to create a no-nonsense sound and bluegrass players go for long, smooth bows. Irish music makes great use of ornamentation, with bow triplets, grace notes, and rolls that are never used in old-time or bluegrass, no matter how fun they are to play. However, some ornaments seem universal; slides fit in everywhere.*

Rhythmic phrasing is also something I listen for. Some fiddle music was originally made for dancing, and you can hear that in the phrasing of Irish and much of the old-time repertoire, although uniquely, Irish often makes use of time signatures like 6/8 or 9/8 that one rarely if ever encounters in old-time. In old-time, the phrasing varies between extremely simple quarter-note patterns and syncopation that would eventually lead to what we hear in ragtime and early jazz. Bluegrass was never intended for dancing and was always about performance and usually for showing off lightning fast techniques. And of course, I listen for the tempo and the dynamics in a style. There is a straightforwardness in most American-style fiddling but subtle variations in Irish music that can be used almost to tell a story.

I suppose I'm lucky that I have the ability to compartmentalize all of these different styles and pull them out when I need them so that a guy like me, raised in northern Indiana and trained classically since age 7, can sound like the various fiddlers who live in my mind, whether from County Clare or the hills of Tennessee.

TOM MORLEY, MULTI-GENRE FIDDLER AND AUTHOR

FOUR WAYS TO LEARN A MELODY

Countless players—even some famous ones—need to prime the pump to get the tune started, and if something goes wrong, tend to return to the beginning as many times as necessary to finally be able to make it all the way through. Or, they might suddenly discover a gaping hole where the melody should be. Does any of this sound familiar?

It's worth taking a moment to examine how, exactly, you learn new tunes, and the skills you can develop to supplement and strengthen your learning process. To assess your learning style, here are a few questions you can ask yourself:

♦ When you learn a new tune, do you tend to forget some or most of the tune you learned afterward?

♦ Can you pick up your instrument and start playing the second half of a tune without playing the A section first?

♦ What happens when you continue to increase your repertoire or skip playing some of your tunes for a stretch of time? Are they still in perfect shape when you come back to them?

Most players apply two common approaches to master new tunes, whether they learn the tune by ear or eye:

Muscle and Auditory Memory through Repetition

There is a tendency to play the tune over and over again sequentially from beginning to end with the expectation that securing the tune into muscle and ears will be enough to lock the tune into place perfectly and permanently. There is nothing inherently wrong with this approach, but without supplemental practice strategies, you are only using a small percentage of your musical brain and ultimately, will not master your tunes as solidly as possible. For instance, anxiety, fatigue, nervousness and/or the passage of time can wipe out muscle memory. And, even if you can still hear the entire tune in your inner ear, it doesn't mean your fingers will remember where to go. You might also learn the first half of the tune better than the second half by always starting at the beginning.

It takes patience to strengthen new learning skills. Try gradually integrating the suggestions offered below into your practice techniques. Ultimately, a complement of these methods will provide a speedier and more thorough mastery over each tune. Mapping the tune as well as developing an understanding of the harmonic support structure will ensure a far more dependable learning process. We will discuss these two aspects of the musical brain below, but first let's determine how well your ears and muscle memory are doing.

Audiation: Hearing the Tune in your Inner Ear

Let's test how well you tend to lock pieces of music into your inner ear.

♦ Choose a tune you think you know really well.

♦ Sing, hum or whistle the entire melody. Take note of the spots that aren't clear or are entirely blank. Your goal is to be able to hear the entire melody start to finish, but eventually you should be able to hear and start playing at any point in the tune. Sound impossible? No worries. You can build these skills over time.

♦ Get ready to play. This time, alternate singing or whistling the melody with playing it. If you aren't able to play the tune from any start point within it, then you are most likely relying too heavily on muscle memory. Make sure to comb through the tune several times, alternating between bow and voice in different spots for various lengths of time: two beats, three, several measures, and so on.

Muscle Memory: Being Able to Play a Tune Automatically While Thinking About Something Entirely Different

While teaching at a fiddle workshop, I used my hour off to listen in on a famous colleague's session. He had chosen the tune he intended to teach well in advance of the event. He'd probably performed it hundreds if not thousands of times. In fact, he'd composed the tune a decade or two earlier. But he had to keep starting at the beginning to find the next phrase in order to teach it.

Muscle memory is an invaluable skill. After all, we don't want to relearn how to get up out of bed every day from scratch. Or how to hold the bow each day as if first starting out. But as in the example above, muscle memory is often the first to disappear when you haven't played a tune for a while, are fatigued, or under stress.

♦ Build on the technique outlined above: alternate singing and playing, but this time play what you've sung. In other words, challenge yourself to hear each phrase of the tune without relying on your instrument: sing or whistle a phrase and then play it, but not just once. Alternate singing and playing each phrase a number of times. This ensures that you've mastered each section for its own sake. This will help you break out of the start-to-finish cycle.

♦ Play through a tune a number of times, but each time, start at a different point within the tune. For instance, start with the B section, or start on the second measure of the tune, or even the last measure of the A section. If you choose a launch point and draw a blank, this is extremely useful information. It means you don't really know each phrase for its own sake, and you're relying entirely on muscle memory with an assist from your ears to carry you through.

Mapping: Picturing all the Muscle Moves without Actually Playing

Your right brain has the ability to generate maps. You should be able to play an entire tune mentally through picturing all the physical moves, but without moving your arms and hands. Once you master this mental "muscle," chances are good you'll be able to play the tune better, faster, and with less effort. This is also a great technique to apply to phrases you habitually blank out on, make mistakes with, or have problems navigating. When you make a mistake, how else might you know whether it was a weakness in the bow hand versus the fingering hand?

- ♦ To test this skill, think of the beginning of a tune you've played many times, close your eyes, and picture playing its opening phrase without moving either hand.

- ♦ Repeat this procedure, but only picture left-hand motion. Then try playing it mentally with just your right hand. If you draw a blank in either case, you have now accessed a crucial clue as to the weak links in your knowledge of the tune. Let's apply these exercises to the opening line in "Beaumont Rag:"

- ♦ For a super challenging exercise, play the pitches in proper order but change the rhythmic values. If you haven't mastered the sequence of pitches, the phrase will fall apart when you change the rhythms. Here's an example:

- ♦ Test your command over the rhythms in the original phrase by altering the pitches.

Lock in the Bare Bones

As discussed earlier, most of us learn tunes as they come: in a linear, sequential fashion from start to finish. But if you highlight the most important pitches from the melody, you'll fortify your knowledge of the tune. It will also make it easier to memorize and build variations. Here is the opening line from "Drowsy Maggie" found in the Celtic section of the book.

Notice how I start with the first note of every measure, followed by each beat to strip the melody down to its essence, lock that into my mind, ears, and muscle memory, and then master the rest of the melody with this through-line as my scaffold.

ARE CHORDS WORTH LEARNING?

Building a Scaffold: Understanding the Harmonic Structure that Supports the Tune

When I first started playing fiddle tunes, I would learn a new tune by playing it over and over again for weeks. One day, I happened to notice the phrase I kept stumbling over was just an upside-down scale right out of the key signature. In other words, the tune was in the key of G, and the line ran down a G major scale. It's just that the phrase didn't start on a G, it started on B: a primary chord tone. And I had practiced G major scales and arpeggios more times than I could count. Once noticed, I never had a problem with the phrase again.

This phrase from our Hungarian tune, "Kettos Jartatoja," is a great example. The tune is in the key of G minor. As long as you know your G minor arpeggio—G, B♭, D—this line is easy to lock in. Consider the difference between learning it note by note versus taking a few seconds to notice that the line starts on the flatted third of the key, dips down one step before running up to the fifth of the key, moves to the second of the key down to the root and up to the flatted third again, and so on until it ends on the root and fifth. Did you just get brain fog? Don't worry. This becomes easier with practice and eventually becomes automatic.

There's a reason why many players warm up with scales and arpeggios. But all too often, they are thought of as just that: a warm-up. Most times, teachers, workshops, and books don't go that extra mile to show you how these warm-ups can serve you as a player. And specifically, how to use this understanding to strengthen and accelerate learning new tunes. An arpeggio outlines the notes of the chord and melodies are built on and around chord tones.

For instance, here's the opening to the bluegrass tune, "Sally Goodin." If you take the time to notice the tune is in the key of A, and the opening starts on the tonic—the root note of the key—then revolves around the root note and its major third, the C#, it will take you far less time to embed the opening into memory.

If you aren't familiar with chords and your brain tends to go on vacation when the topic comes up, you may have a strong urge to skip to the next section of this book. Think of the chords for a tune like a scaffold. They support the melody and add motion to the feel of the tune while fleshing it out. The good news? Fiddle tunes don't utilize many chords and they tend to favor the same keys: G, A, D, and E with occasional journeys into C and F. Blues, swing and jazz are more complex art forms that do require a knowledge of and dexterity in all twelve keys, but you can always start with the keys that are more familiar—particularly for the blues, which applies the same harmonic template to the key of your choice.

It's helpful to understand that three-part chords define a triad: root, third and fifth. This simpler chord form is more commonly used in roots styles. Four-part chords, popular in blues, swing and jazz are made up of the root, third and fifth with an additional note on top: either the sixth or the seventh. Four-part chords contribute a spicier sound and determine the type of seventh you'll use in the scale—flatted or major.

Three-Part Chords

Once you learn major and minor in these primary keys, it's easy to add a sixth or seventh on top. It's just a question of whether the seventh is major (Cmaj7) or flatted (C7).

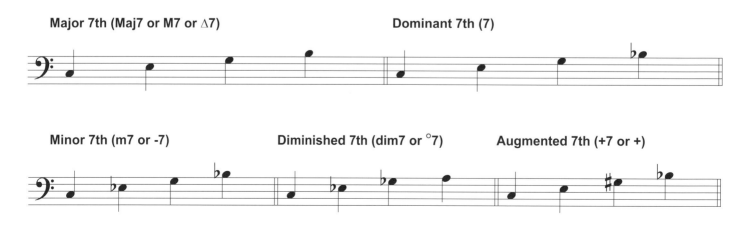

There are additional four-part chords: major sixth or M6 (1 3 5 6), minor sixth or m6 (1 ♭3 5 6), and minor major or minMaj, -Δ7, mM (1 ♭3 5 7).

The chord symbol tells us the kind of scale we can use. Roots music often employs chords that favor the use of the same scale throughout, so if you want to improvise or create variations on the melody, you can restrict yourself to the notes in the key signature or the pitches outlined by the melody.

Why bother to learn the chords if you know that you can just use your ears to steer your note choices? Well, when you get on a horse to ride a trail, if you look at a nice flower garden on your right, the horse will start to move in that direction, even if you didn't signal it with the reins. The brain operates in a similar fashion.

G Major chord tones and scale:

A minor chord tones and scale:

If you think "G major scale" because of the key signature, your fingers will tend to run up and down G to G, you'll probably favor the G string, and your ideas might become boring. But if you think "G major arpeggio followed by A minor arpeggio," even though they share the same scale, your fingers will navigate an entirely different pathway and convey a fresh series of ideas, when you picture each tonal map.

For a thorough explanation of chords and scales, see my Hal Leonard books, *Improvising Violin* (HL00695234) and *The Contemporary Violinist* (HL00695420).

THE ART OF ACCOMPANIMENT

COMPING AND SECONDING

Western Swing, Cajun, and Swedish fiddle styles, in particular, include a second bowed string part that harmonizes with and/or rhythmically supports the melody. But you can carry these skills into any style. The simplest possibility is to play the melody an octave above or below the main melody to fatten it up. Here's an example of the melody a third below:

You can travel parallel to the melody a third above or a sixth below or alternate between an octave apart with a third above or below to generate a harmony part. Ironically, a third above or below is actually the same pitch, but yields an entirely different results. For instance, B is a third above a G; a B can also be found a sixth below the G.

You can also use the notes of the chords to accompany the melody. The opening to "Blues at Dawn" uses a G7 chord: G B D and F♮. Notice how I've used notes from the G7 chord to accompany the melody.

Try adding a rhythmic accompaniment by cloning the primary rhythmic groove found in the tune or musical style and use the notes of the chords to play backup. In this case, since it's a bluegrass tune, "Sally Goodin," I've used the rhythmic drive from the shuffle stroke for the chordal accompaniment. You can always add double-stops that are made up of combinations of the chord tones: A, C♯, and E.

In general, it's much easier to develop an accompaniment if you record yourself playing the lead melody slowly and then play it back to experiment with ideas. Start simple and add on as you feel comfortable. If you like how it sounds, chances are good everyone else will enjoy your accompaniment as well.

BASS LINES

It's well worth your time and effort to learn how to generate a bass line. The bass line culls its notes from the chords. And for fiddle tunes, it's easy to come up with a simple bass part.

As long as you know the root and fifth of the key, you can immediately alternate between those two notes. Here's an example in the key of A:

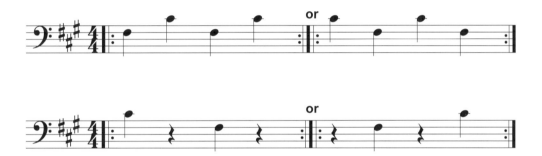

It's true that many styles require more complex bass lines, but if you start with the basics, you can build from there. The key is to listen to the rhythmic preferences as expressed in the melody and try to imitate bass lines on recordings in that style.

Is There Only One Right Way to Play a Bass Line?

Absolutely not. There are a number of options. The best course of action is to listen to as many examples of the style as you can, and then experiment with ideas.

Bass Lines Can Provide a Wider Range of Skills

When you go to a jam session or play with a friend, it can be fun to alternate between playing an accompaniment or the melody. At a session, if someone starts up a tune you aren't familiar with, you won't have to sit it out. You'll have honed the skills to play a bass line or an interesting backing line. As mentioned earlier, fiddle tunes tend to favor a small number of keys, so you won't have to worry about suddenly having to come up with a bass line in the key of D♭, so you might consider starting with roots styles before you attempt to develop a bass line for styles like blues, swing or jazz.

To build a bass line that's more complex than the root and fifth, you will need to know the notes for each chord. For instance, if you see the chord symbol, C7, and know the root (C), third (E), fifth (G) and flatted seventh (B♭), you can come up with a number of combinations of those notes. You might opt for quarter notes that land on the beat, dotted rhythms, or syncopated figures, depending on the style.

Notice how some of the chromatic tones in this bass line for "Beaumont Rag" lead to primary chord tones:

By contrast, a tune from Eastern Europe, might only use the root of the key with a trickier rhythmic figure:

Ensemble Skills

When we learn how to participate in the role the rhythm section plays, we improve our participation in the ensemble. This is because our ears tend to ignore or minimize everything but the melody. By learning to play a bass line, we are able to truly hear and understand everything the bass player contributes to the group. We can then interact with him or her by piggybacking rhythmic ideas or mimicking and embellishing on a line we hear from the bass. As far as our ears are concerned, the bass player is no longer a "metronome" in the background, but an equal partner in the ensemble.

Arrangements

As your ability to play improves, it's natural to seek area players and join into or start your own group. Learning about chords and bass lines will enable you to provide accurate and even creative suggestions to the guitarist, keyboard and/or bass player. It will also enable you to decipher moments within the tune when the rhythm section is wrong or making weaker choices, correct them, and improve the group sound.

And this leads us to another important topic...

ARRANGEMENTS OF TUNES

If you are considering forming a group or are already a member of one, it's important to learn to cultivate your ability to generate interesting arrangements for the tunes in your repertoire. Fiddle tunes are short and often fast-paced, so they tend to whirl by. Learning to create medleys of tunes is an important skill to get started. There are no clear-cut rules for how to go about organizing a medley, but here are some suggestions.

♦ Select a group of tunes that are in the same key and play each tune anywhere between two to four times before transitioning to the next one, and the next. Or, purposefully select tunes that are in neighboring keys to build more variety. For instance, you could step up from the key of D to a tune in E and then F. Or stick with keys that share common chords, like the key of G followed by the key of D, since D is the fifth of the key of G.

♦ Choose a tune that favors the lower pitches on your instrument and follow it with one that goes up higher to help build energy.

♦ Start with a slow tune—or play it slowly—and gradually work up speed each time you transition to the next tune in your medley and the next.

♦ Play the first tune by yourself, then add instruments into the arrangement each time you make the changeover to a new tune, so the full band sound is reached by the last tune.

Certain styles, like Irish and Appalachian, are receptive to personalized variations of the melody. Other styles, like the blues or Gypsy jazz, call upon the player to generate their own ideas after the melody has been played. Many of the skills required by each approach are similar, if not the same. Let's look at this in greater depth.

As a long-time back-of-the-orchestra second violinist, I've discovered that it's just as much fun to accompany a fiddle tune with some cool backup licks, counter lines, and chordy rhythm stuff as it is to actually play the tune. I'd recommend

learning some chords and simple chord progressions, as there are really not that many. Start by finding some I (one), IV (four), and V (five) sounds in the popular fiddle keys.

I'm happy to inform you, from my extensive research at Berklee College and at fiddle festivals around the world, that just about every existing chord can be expressed, in its essence, on the bottom two strings of your instrument…in first position. That's good news! And of course, a little rhythm, whether you're chopping, or just bouncing along at the bow's balance point on one lonesome note, really sets those fancy melodies off something fierce. The more tunes you learn, the more you'll see that there are just a few rhythm chord patterns that can be used over and over.

When you learn that next tune, make sure you get an idea of what the chords might be, and remember that many styles of fiddling have very flexible rules for what the chords are!

DAROL ANGER, MULTI-GENRE FIDDLER, COMPOSER AND PERFORMER

HOW TO GENERATE VARIATIONS

It's much easier to invent variations on melody lines or generate solos when you have already mastered the harmonic support structure that underpins the melody.

For instance, here's the opening to "Beaumont Rag" followed by a variation. Notice how the notes weave around the primary melody and use the chord tones for C7 (C, E, G, B♭), with some chromatic passing tones that help move the line.

Permutations

I've borrowed the term "permutations" from mathematics to describe the resequencing of pitches. There are several steps involved when permuting a group of pitches.

♦ Use the notes of the melody to generate a map of the primary pitches available to you. Sometimes this information can be derived from the key signature, but not always. For instance, the tune may use a pentatonic (five-note) scale, or the key signature might lead you to believe you are in a major key, when in fact, the melody is built on a minor scale. How will you know? Trust your ears. They will always lead you to the correct tonal map. The only advantage to mastering this aspect of music theory, is that you can often grasp the map more quickly. For instance, if the key signature has one sharp, I might immediately assume I'm in the key of G. But when I look at the melody and chords, if the melody ends on an E with an Em chord and I know that the relative minor is found a sixth above the major (your instrument is tuned in fifths, so picture your open D string and up a whole step to find the sixth of G), then I can immediately solo using the E minor scale rather than tinkering around in G and sounding okay, but not quite right.

♦ Practice the tonal map by playing the notes in order, from bottom to top and back down again. Notice how I haven't used the word "scale" because the melody may avoid some of the seven pitches found in a scale. For instance, the two sharps in the key signature for the tune "Drowsy Maggie" tell me I'm in the key of D, but the melody revolves around an E in the A section of the tune. My ears will eventually lead me to E minor, but as long as I know that the Dorian mode, 1 2 ♭3 4 5 6 ♭7, can be found on the second degree of a major scale, I can save a good deal of time and practice the correct map.

♦ Rearrange the order of the notes in as many configurations as you can. Feel free to use walking quarter notes to accomplish this, or borrow a rhythm from the tune.

So, what's the point? You are teaching yourself how to spot pitches that are central to the melody and learning to manipulate them to create variations. This is how you can individualize your version of the tune and/or improvise after playing the melody if desired.

Time Increments

It's essential to be able to hear how each musical phrase fits into its prescribed time-window so you can replace the written line with a polished variation or an original idea. For instance, if a musical phrase lasts four beats or four measures and you don't know how to shape your line to fit into that time increment, no matter how cool your idea is, it won't communicate well.

There are many professions that require the ability to track time accurately without looking at a clock. In basketball, the athlete only has five seconds to inbound the ball. In the restaurant business, the chef must track the three-minute egg at the same time as a twelve-minute dish, while starting yet another dish from scratch. This is a discrete "brain muscle" that requires dedicated practice.

To get started, it's best to use a backing track that holds you to the meter you've chosen. Let's say you want to master a four-beat time increment. You can use an app or software program and set it up to repeat an accompaniment in the style that interests you. In workshops, I often use a four-beat phrase with a rhythmic placeholder. I partner everyone in groups of two. One partner plays the rhythmic figure and the other plays fillers. Then they switch. But this can be done with a recording device or by alternating between a rhythmic jumping-off point and a filler. The idea is to learn to create an idea that fulfills the rest of the measure with a clean ending before the downbeat of the next measure. The pitch used for accompaniment can be determined by the key you want to play in.

Here's an example using the opening melody of "Kitchen Girl." Notice how we start with the "bare bones" melody and explore variations that start and end on the same pitches as the melody as a technique designed to frame the time increment. Later, you can stray outside these designated pitches. Notice how I've included accents and bowings to perpetuate the stylistic flavor of the tune.

Melody

Variations

Longer Forms

There are a number of styles that will call on you to lock in longer time increments, like twelve bars for the blues, or thirty-two bars for jazz tunes. It's essential to use a backing track for support. Start with smaller increments, like one measure, four measures, then eight, and so on.

Rhythmic Cloning

We have just discussed excerpting pitches from a tune you're working on to practice mastering its notes in a number of configurations toward creating more interesting, well-timed variations and improvisations. You can also excerpt the primary rhythms from the tune and apply each rhythmic unit to the notes you've extracted from the tune. Here's an example using the opening to "Kitchen Girl:" the same rhythmic values are coupled with pitch permutations.

Ordinarily, when we set out to create a variation or solo, we tend to pay far more attention to directing the left hand, while the right is given a "good luck, you're on your own" send-off, so it tends to follow along or turn to ingrained habits.

Since the rhythmic centers of the brain are positioned in locations independent of the centers that track pitch and melody, it's useful to focus on each skill set separately.

Try excerpting a key rhythm phrase from a tune you're working on and apply it to each pitch you've extracted from the melody. Work this over the full range of your instrument before introducing the next rhythmic phrase. This is particularly useful when learning a new style, because this process helps imprint the rhythmic signature of the genre into auditory and muscle memory. You can also excerpt a rhythmic motif from a tune and substitute new pitches from the tune's key signature while maintaining the rhythmic line. This practice approach also provides ideas to use for a harmony line. Here's a phrase from "Polska efter Pelle Fors." Traditionally speaking, the fiddler would not improvise on a Swedish tune after stating the melody but but they would certainly play a harmony line.

Melody

Identical rhythmic phrase played a third above

Cadences as a Learning Tool

Most tunes include a short musical idea that broadcasts the ending of the tune, or a section of the tune. The motion of the pitches and the chords work together to make it clear that the melody is coming to a close. It's far easier to build the skills we've discussed above by developing improvisational skills within this small musical container. Extract a one- or two-bar cadence from the tune you're currently working on. Use an app or software program to generate that part of the melody and/or chords, set it up to repeat a number of times, and practice originating ideas against the accompaniment.

Here are some examples from tunes in this book that are coordinated with backing tracks included with the book's online media. This first one includes four ideas built on the two-bar melody that closes out the A and B sections of the bluegrass tune, "Sally Goodin":

CADENCES

"Sally Goodin" Cadence

"Kitchen Girl" Cadence

"The Shetland Fiddler" Cadence

"Reel de Remi" Cadence

One of the fun aspects to this practice approach is that you can extract the closing phrase from any style of music, including classical, and figure out the chords by looking at the key signature. If the key signature places the tune in D, invariably, the line will end on a D. There are, of course, exceptions to this, but your ears will always tell you when you're right or wrong.

This is a gentle and helpful way to learn more about music theory, because there is normally a tension and release at the end of each tune. A dominant seventh (V7) chord creates tension that naturally leads to resolution on the one (I) chord. Your instrument is tuned in fifths which makes it easy to figure out the five (V) chord since it can be found straight across on the next highest string, but you will have to learn about key signatures. The good news? Fiddle tunes, no matter which genre, tend to stick to keys like G (one sharp: F#), D (F#, C#), and A (F#, C#, G#). Occasionally, you'll come across a tune in F (Bb) or Bb (Bb, Eb).

Major Keys and Their Key Signatures

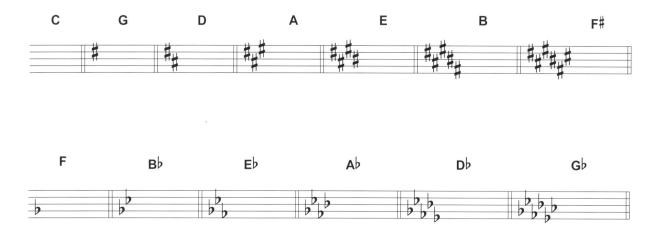

Rhythmic Preferences

Every culture has developed its own rhythmic language. While you might argue that all music is made up of the basic rhythms, and you'd be right, each genre tends to work those rhythms in a different sequence. And they might favor some rhythmic values over others. When we figure in the use of accents, slurs, and ornamentation, the distinction between styles widens.

Bowed string players, when learning new melodies, tend to listen more carefully for the sequence of pitches. They capture the rhythms tangentially along the way. To even out your skills, try focusing on the rhythmic signature of each tune you learn equal to the motion of the pitches. Ultimately, when you learn a tune, you should be able to bow the rhythms on an open string while hearing the melodic motion in your inner ear. When you unglue the rhythmic language of the tune from the melodic language, master each, then join them back together, you will play the tune with far more conviction and accuracy and remember it with improved clarity.

First, make sure you can play each of the basic rhythms accurately.

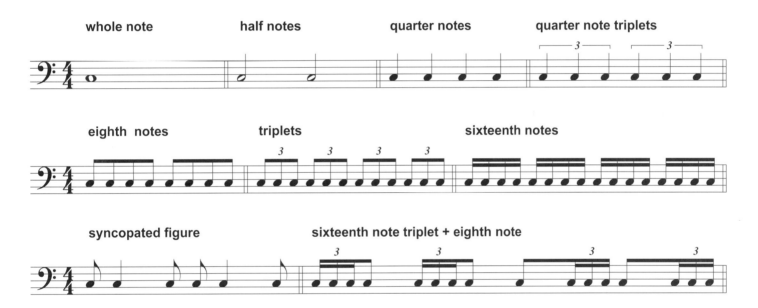

More complex styles, like the blues or jazz, can work a far wider range of rhythmic ideas, and every tune contains variations despite its disposition toward certain rhythms, so keep this in mind as we proceed. To focus exclusively on the rhythmic centers of the brain as well as right-hand coordination, try bowing the rhythms for each tune in this book on an open string. Since some of the rhythmic ideas rely on the application of a slur to certain groupings, try applying a subtle pause between slurred notes.

To develop additional rhythmic skills, see my Hal Leonard DVD, *Rhythmizing the Bow* (HL00320461).

ADDITIONAL TECHNIQUES

STRING CROSSING

Every style of music requires the navigation of the bow across all four strings. But certain roots styles amplify this technique through repetitive motion between two strings.

This first example is from the Irish tune, "Drowsy Maggie." Notice the accented notes on the moving pitches, not the repeated E, which is called a *pedal point*. If you let your elbow fall into gravity on each string crossing, you'll be able to generate a natural accentuation of the moving pitches on the A string.

You will produce a more accurate sound and ergonomic muscle response if you understand when to pivot your forearm by leaving your elbow halfway between the two strings, versus when to use your elbow to alternate strings. In part, this should be determined by how fast you are playing and whether or not you want to accentuate one string more than the other. Practice both types of motion and consciously choose one above the other based on ease of movement and best sound.

This next example demonstrates how the "bare bones" line in "Beaumont Rag" from the B section, can be dressed up with a bowing called the *double shuffle*.

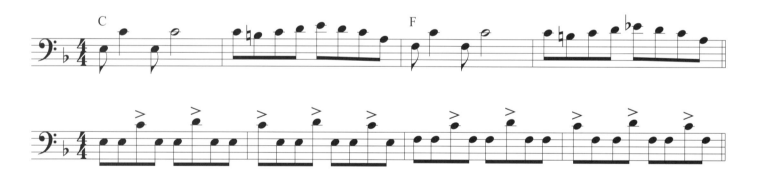

ORNAMENTATION

Each of us selects clothing that reflects our favored styles and colors. The same applies to culture and sound. Why does an Irish tune place the grace note above the core pitch, whereas Cajun tends to position the grace note from below the core pitch? Why do some styles embrace vibrato while others reject it? Why a turn versus a flick? Or a bowed treble versus a shimmer? The same answer could apply to why some people prefer peppermint ice cream over chocolate, though in some cases, the fiddle is imitating the vocal style or an instrument of that culture. For instance, the Irish or Scottish bagpipes, or a particular speech pattern in Sweden, where the voice (and bow) includes a surge after the halfway point of certain vowels or longer tones.

Left-hand Ornamentation

Think of a stand-alone note, and then ask yourself: how can I "dress up" this note? You will probably find any sound you can possibly invent somewhere on this planet in one musical style or another. Generally, ornaments are added to held notes rather than faster-moving values, like eighths, triplets, or sixteenths for practical reasons; there usually isn't enough time to include extras to faster rhythms.

We don't speak in a monotone voice (at least I hope not) and ornaments add a great deal of expression and interest to the ride of the melody. Here are a few examples:

Right-hand Ornamentation

The bow-hand can also ornament a note. Sometimes it's subtle, like a swell halfway into the pitch or just before it ends. There are also fancier colorations as demonstrated in the video tutorial.

Note: *Appropriate ornamentation will be supplied as it pertains to each style throughout the book.*

ORNAMENTATION

DOUBLE STOPS

Styles like Appalachian and bluegrass call for sounding out two notes together, and there are a few simple procedures you can use to improve how you play double stops.

♦ Make sure to position your right elbow halfway between the two strings.

♦ To start, draw smaller bows, since elbow height will have to incrementally shift up or down when you power longer bows, which will add to the technical challenge.

♦ Let your bow arm release into gravity to achieve a full sound rather than muscling the bow into the string.

AMPLIFICATION

There could be situations in the future when you will need amplification. It's important to understand when to choose a microphone on a stand, a clip-on versus built-in technology that attaches to your tailpiece, bridge or soundpost, or a solid-body instrument that has little or no sound when played "acoustically."

Think of the amplification system on your instrument like owning an ignition key, but no car. In all cases, except in a club that has its own sound system, you will also need an amp to amplify your instrument.

For home practice or in a traditional session where equality is more appropriate, you can play on your acoustic instrument without a worry. However, here are a few instances when you will most likely require a boost to your signal:

♦ If you perform with a full band, you likely won't be heard without amplification.

♦ Some jam sessions include an excessive number of rhythm instruments. Maybe you're the only bowed string player that shows up and you can't even hear yourself play. Without amplification, you might be tempted to press down harder with your bow. This will signal the left hand to exert excessive pressure and you'll most likely struggle to play fast, leaving the session tired, sore, injured, or all three.

♦ Acoustically speaking, some performance venues weren't designed for music or weren't configured to support acoustic instruments. It's the difference between playing in a bathroom versus a closet stuffed with clothing. Let's say you've rehearsed with a guitarist at home and the balance was perfect. But then you have an opportunity to perform in a church, a large hall, or a small club and can't hear yourself properly or—just as bad—the audience can't hear you.

♦ If you would like to experiment with any of the many special effects on the market, like the looper, phase shifter, wah-wah, or reverb, you will need an amplified instrument.

"Be prepared for all eventualities…" is a handy motto to live by. Better that your equipment sits in the trunk of your car or off to the side of the stage than at home, and all your practice and preparation is for naught.

What Should You Buy and Why?

Today, there are many amplification solutions available to bowed strings players. As you research mics, make sure whatever you buy has been specifically developed for bowed strings. The electronics configured for a singer are completely different than for violin, viola or cello. Think about the issue of mobility as well. Do you want to be locked into standing in the same position to play through a mic, or do you want to gift yourself with the mobility a clip-on mic can provide?

If you use a mic—on a stand or clipped onto your instrument—you will have to be extremely careful about where you stand because if you accidentally angle it to face the amp, you can generate loud feedback. You might also pick up the sounds of the other musicians. A pickup system built into the bridge or installed inside your instrument will provide you with physical freedom in rehearsals and performances.

To use electronic effects, it's best to buy a solid-body instrument. A solid-body avoids the problem of hearing one sound through the amp doubled by an acoustic sound in the room, since the solid-body is barely audible unless plugged into an amp. Its electronics super-charge the output so that you get the best possible version of whichever special effects you use.

No matter which option you ultimately choose, you will need some cables to attach your equipment to your amp and/or electronic effects. Most instruments will require a 1/4" guitar plug.

I like to plug an elbow-shaped cable into my instrument so that it doesn't stick into me and then use the straight-edged side to plug into a stomp box or amp. Add an extra cable for each special effects box. For instance, one cable from your instrument to the first stomp box, a second from that box to the next, and so on.

PLAYING IN A GROUP

JAM SESSIONS

What to Play if You Don't Know the Melody

For those of you who attend jam sessions regularly, you already know it's a gamble as to whether or not you'll already know every tune that's suggested. Depending on how the session is organized, folks can take turns suggesting tunes or the leader will be in charge of the selection. So how do you participate in either scenario if you don't know the melody?

◆ Find the tonal center (the key).

◆ Use pizzicato to figure out the notes of the scale. Is the tune in a major key (1-2-3-4-5-6-7), natural minor (1-2-♭3-4-5-♭6-♭7) or modal? If modal, more likely than not, it will be the dorian mode (1-2-♭3-4-5-6-♭7) or the mixolydian mode (1-2-3-4-5-6-♭7).

◆ Identify the primary rhythmic feel and use primary notes, starting with the tonic, to create a rhythmic/harmonic accompaniment. Then, keep your ears fixed on the melody to weave in notes or phrases until you've picked up the entire tune and can join in on the melody.

Tempo and Volume

If the group is playing faster than you can, rather than building bad habits, try catching the first note or notes of each measure or play an accompaniment if you don't feel comfortable asking everyone to slow down. Technical issues you could have spent weeks working on can fall apart and make for an incredibly uncomfortable musical experience and you might find yourself holding your breath and/or tensing up.

It's pretty common for each musician to play louder to hear him or herself, which pushes the volume of the entire group up incrementally. If necessary, try changing your position in the room to hear yourself better without intensifying left- and right-hand pressure into the strings.

PLAYING IN A BAND

Over the years, I've coached hundreds of students through cruddy band experiences: power struggles, broken promises, dictatorship versus group consensus, and so on.

Before you say "yes" to playing in a band, make sure you understand how the band leader prefers to develop arrangements of material and the role you will and won't be allowed to play in the group. Be clear about what you want from the experience and, if agreed upon, hold your ground if you find agreements tread upon. Here are a few topics worth covering:

◆ Whether or not you can expect equity between band members as regards financial renumeration and input.

◆ Amount of time expected of you per week or month.

◆ How much control you will or won't have over your musical contributions to the band.

VIOLA AND CELLO: AN OVERVIEW

It might seem to you violists and cellists as though every single bowed string style in the world only features or includes the violin/fiddle, but that isn't true.

Viola

The viola has played a role in traditional music in Eastern Europe, most notably, in Transylvania as well as Romania, Slovakia and Hungary. The instrument is often altered for use in folk bands by only utilizing three strings, G, D and A, with a flattened bridge for rhythmic double-stops, referred to as a *kontra* or *brácsa*. The A string is sometimes tuned down an octave to handle bass lines.

In Sweden, probably because of its close relationship to the traditional instrument, the *nyckelharpa*, some violas are tuned C-D-C-A while the others are tuned in fifths: C-G-D-A like Western viola tuning.

Today's multi-genre violists such as David Wallace, Tanya Kalmanovitch, Mat Maneri, Martha Mooke, Leanne Darling, and others, are stretching the boundaries of the instrument's role in styles such as jazz, rock, roots music, Arabic, and electro-acoustic music.

I grew up in the Canadian North, where the fiddler was someone special: a convener of people and culture. When we moved south in the early 1980s, I  *joined a group called the Calgary Fiddlers. I learned many different styles, but when I switched to viola I had to find my own sound. It took a leap of imagination to hear the viola as a jazz instrument, because there were no models. But that was actually an asset, because I had the rare opportunity to create a sound that people had never heard before. Over the course of my professional life, I've seen time and again how value and innovations comes from the margins—from people we haven't yet heard from.*

I want to remind you that you don't need permission to make music. You don't need to win an audition or a competition or a grant. You don't need a degree from a music school, or the right friends in the right places, or a life in a glittering cultural capital, or the touch of some divine inspiration, or an otherworldly talent, or someone powerful to declare that you are "good enough" to "make it".

You are good enough, already.

Whoever you are, wherever you are, there is a sound that only you can make and you can make it anytime you want. We need you to make that sound.

TAYNA KALMANOVITCH, IMPROVISING VIOLIST

Cello

While in my early teens, I studied dance at Connecticut College American Dance Festival. My world was turned upside down by cellist Gwendolyn Watson. She'd been hired to accompany dance classes and improvised wildly, using every sound available on the instrument and then some. I had my violin with me and she enlisted me to join her. Her fertile imagination on the cello inspired me to dip my toes into free improvisation. I even ended up performing with her to accompany a famous dance company. The scales were forever tipped and I returned home far more interested in pursuing music than dance.

My next encounter with "alternative" cello was back in the 1970s. Jay Ungar's band "The Putnam String County Band," included cellist Abby Newton. This group focused on old-time—or old-timey as they called it—music. In that context, I heard Abby move agilely between bass lines, chords, and melody. Years later, I met cellist David Darling through saxophonist and world music proponent, Paul Winter. David brought yet another voice onto the cello as a composer and improviser. He and cellist Eugene Friesen have forged paths in world music styles through their work with the Paul Winter Consort and thereafter.

Historically speaking, the cello was adopted by many Romani musicians to play bass lines and rhythmic accompaniments. It has also played a role in old-time music, Scottish, and jazz, among other styles.

Other cellists of note include Natalie Haas and Liz Davis Maxfield in the Celtic style, Sean Grissom, Cajun music, co-founder of the String Project LA, Jacob Szekely, and multi-genre player Mike Block. These artists adeptly alternate between melody, harmony, and rhythm, employing traditional and contemporary techniques.

There are also a number of rock cellists featured in groups like Cello Fury, Rasputin and Apocalyptica. Jazz cellists of particular note are Abdul Wadud, Diedre Murray, Ron Carter, and Dave Holland, to name a few.

While living next door to Jay Ungar and Lyn Hardy in the mid 1970s, they invited me to join their square dance band. Through them, I met John Cohen of the New Lost City Ramblers, who showed me photos of cellos in old timey string bands

 *from the early 1900s. We formed the Putnam String County Band within which I focused on recreating the sound of the cello in old time style as we toured over the next few years. During that time, I met Scottish singer, Jean Redpath, at one of the festivals we were both playing. She asked me to record on her next album at Philo Records. This was the beginning of a thirty-year friendship and musical collaboration including seventeen CDs. During my tours with Jean, I spent quite a bit of time in Scotland, where I discovered that the cello had been used as a traditional music instrument, playing the airs and dances alongside fiddlers. There is a painting in the National Gallery of the famous Scottish fiddler and composer, Neil Gow, with his brother on cello playing for a country dance in the Scottish Highlands. I was honored to bring the cello back into both American and Scottish traditional music.*

ABBY NEWTON, CELLIST AND AUTHOR

AMERICAN ROOTS STYLES

~ Old-Time/Appalachian

~ Bluegrass

~ Cajun

~ Franco-American

~ Western Swing

INTRODUCTION

Generations of fiddlers gradually morphed their skills and repertoire into an impressive array of new styles once on American soil. Fiddlers combined repertoire, dance rhythms, ornamentation, and techniques imported from England, Ireland, Scotland, France, and Africa.

This point is so important, it bears repeating. For the most part, fiddlers invented just about every new American style: Appalachian, also referred to as old-time, bluegrass, Cajun, Franco-American, and Western Swing. Afro-American fiddlers and vocalists also created the blues, followed by offspring like boogie-woogie, ragtime, R&B, swing, and rock. Though each genre represents the uniqueness of a living culture, it also reflects a willingness on the part of musicians to explore and create new sounds while simultaneously preserving history.

The Apache fiddle's name, tsíí' edo'a'tl, means "wood that sings" or "singing wood." Prior to the European invasion that began with Christopher Columbus in 1492, well over 550 different tribes inhabited America. Their music was (and is) vocal and often accompanied by instruments such as rattles, flutes, whistles, drums and other percussion. Only one tribe, the indigenous Apache of the southwestern United States, adopted the violin into their music.

I'm fascinated by the different ways musicians bring tunes to life, imbuing them with swing, with groove, with tradition, and with surprises; all the while warming the hearts of listeners and animating the feet of dancers. There were inspiring times when I focused on just one fiddle style—bluegrass, old-time, Irish, swing, Klezmer, and New England. But the varied techniques and approaches I encountered in drifting through multiple styles have broadened my perspective, sharpened my ear, improved my improvising and tune writing, and led me to meet and appreciate many more people as mentors, as jamming buddies, and as fellow performers. Imagine yourself doing the same!

DAVE REINER, FOUNDER, FIDDLE HELL MASSACHUSETTS FESTIVAL

OLD-TIME/APPALACHIAN

The term "Appalachia" refers to a wide expanse of states covering roughly 200,000 square miles, not just the southeastern region as is commonly thought. The traditional music of Appalachia was imported from Ireland, England, Scotland, and Africa. Old-time fiddling represents a slow evolution over several centuries of Anglo-Celtic ballads, instrumental dance music, and spiritual hymns that gradually melded to create a new art form, old-time, also referred to as *old-timey*, *hillbilly*, *mountain music* and *Appalachian fiddling*. It's impossible to know the exact date old-time fiddling came into its own. Since tunes were taught by ear and passed from generation to generation, the earliest documentation started after the invention of recorded music in 1925, and notation of some of these tunes took another forty years or so.

There are hundreds, if not thousands of tunes in everyday use across the country, all learned by ear, with some tunes favored over others. If you master a handful of the more popular tunes, you can go anywhere in America and find musicians to play with. Though called *traditional* or *public domain* because the composers are unknown, each tune has mutated over the years, depending on the memory and playing skills of the fiddler, so it's nearly impossible to determine the original version.

Some of the more commonly played tunes include: "The Arkansas Traveler," "Solder's Joy," "Boil 'em Cabbage Down," "Cripple Creek," "Old Joe Clarke," "Red Wing," "Liberty," "Angeline the Baker," "Katy Hill," "Sally Goodin," "Ragtime Annie," "Devil's Dream," and "Blackberry Blossom."

Almost every Appalachian tune follows a traditional form: there is an A section that repeats, followed by a B section that repeats. Depending on how the tune is notated, each section is usually either four or eight bars in length, though there are some exceptions, called "crooked tunes." Most of these tunes have a question and answer feel to them. The melody will pose an idea that begs for follow-up, and the second half will provide the response.

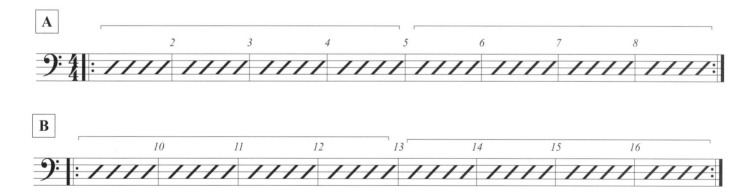

The Rhythmic Dance

The energetic groove that underlies this style emphasizes the second and fourth beats of the measure. The primary bow technique, called *shuffle stroke*, creates a danceable, rhythmic drive. Even when shuffle stroke isn't applied, it's always heard by the player and implied throughout, despite alternative bow patterns. Here are a few steps you can take to embed the correct feel into your bow hand and ears:

Turn on a metronome or a recording of an Appalachian tune to establish the walking pulse. Count out the beats, "one, **two**, three, **four**," and then gradually avoid saying "one" or "three," so you're only counting on the second and fourth beats.

Next, cover your strings with the palm of your left hand to avoid sounding out any pitches. Use the center of your bow to create a drum-like hit by dropping it on the strings to percussively sound out the second and fourth beats. In the early days of bluegrass, this bow-stroke was called *chunk* or *chunking*.

Keep this sound in your ears as you progress into the shuffle stroke. Notice how the long bow does not receive the accent. It's the first of the two short bows. This is the basic move, but keep in mind there are subtle distinctions as played by each regional group of old-time players.

Choose a group of notes from a scale or a melody and practice applying the shuffle stroke to those notes. Repeat a number of times to help lock this into your bowing arm. Here is shuffle stroke as applied to the first of two tonal maps you will need in a moment. Notice how the shuffle stroke is configured for constantly moving eighth notes in the second example.

We will focus on a commonly known tune, "Kitchen Girl." It is a modal tune. This term is commonly used when referring to melodies that are based on a scale with a flatted seventh, as is the case in the A section of this tune as shown above.

Then, the tune changes to minor by flatting the third of the key for the B section. This transition adds spice to the overall quality of the tune. In modal language, the tune starts out in the *Mixolydian* mode and transitions to the *Dorian* mode.

Once you've locked in the melody, come up with some variations of your own. Here is one of many possible variations for the first two measures of the melody.

This first version of "Kitchen Girl" is what I call the "bare bones" melody. The second version adds the shuffle stroke with some extra flourishes. This is to demonstrate how you can add your own individualized touch to the rendition of any old-time tune.

Kitchen Girl

🔊 BACKING TRACK

The embedded, unique rhythms of old-time fiddling make up the engine that propels the style. Pay close attention to that aspect of this giant deep well of tunes and songs, and this book will open some important doors! Listen to the old masters, and it all starts to make sense!

BRUCE MOLSKY, OLD-TIME MUSICIAN AND ROOTS EDUCATOR

Kitchen Girl

In the early sixties, I set out on a mission to find and record old-time fiddle players of the upper South. The fiddle players I recorded were all white fiddle players, mostly old men in the 1960s. The more I studied the style, the more I realized that the bowing patterns of all the fiddlers I visited were filled with complicated, elaborate syncopations. Those syncopations were not something they added into their music just to make it lively. It was their music. That was the way they thought music. It was embedded very deeply in their style. And these were men who had learned to play the fiddle in the late 19th century…before jazz, before blues, even before ragtime. So syncopation was not something they learned from popular music or from the modern 20th century forms of syncopation that we all know. Where I think they learned it was from the black fiddlers who participated deeply in the tradition of fiddling in the early 19th century. Blacks participated in the very creation of the style of fiddling we now think of as Southern fiddling. It's clear that no other part of the English speaking world has these complicated syncopated patterns. It's an Afro-American contribution to this fiddling style. Then blacks dropped out of fiddling in the later 19th century, went on to guitar and keyboard and other instruments. Whites continued the tradition, but by then, it was a tradition that was equally Anglo-American and Afro-American, a tradition that was brought together on American soil, the best of Europe and the best of Africa, and in certain ways, I might add, certain elements that you might call the best of the "New World." It's a deeply American art, blending together into a new creative form.

ALAN JABBOUR, FORMER DIRECTOR NATIONAL FOLKLIFE, **1989** INTERVIEW

BLUEGRASS

A number of old-time tunes can be found in the bluegrass repertoire. That's because this style came from the same source. Bluegrass founder Bill Monroe grew up on Appalachian ballads and Appalachian instrumental music that featured the fiddle with Dobro and guitar. The bluegrass sound also includes mandolin as well as a specific rapid finger-picking style applied to the banjo through a combination of the thumb, middle and index fingers.

Monroe loved to listen to the blues, a style that embraces improvisation. Unlike old-time music, bluegrass also includes solos, commonly referred to as *breaks* in bluegrass. You will find tips on how to create variations and improvise in the opening material of this book.

Like old-time fiddling, bluegrass repertoire is huge, and the two styles also share a number of tunes. Here's a partial list of some of the most popular fiddle tunes in this style: "Red-Haired Boy," "Jerusalem Ridge," "Bill Cheatum," "Red Wing," "Billy in the Lowground," "Old Joe Clarke," "Over the Waterfall," "Shady Grove," and "Black Mountain Rag."

So, what is the difference between the old-time fiddle style and bluegrass fiddling? For one thing, this style includes more complex double-stops than old-time fiddling, which uses mostly open strings to drone against. In addition to taking solos, players tend to build on simple melodies to create fast-moving lines that twist and turn. You will also find more daring sonorities. For instance, instead of an A, C# or E against an open A string, the double stops often include more complex harmonies, like a C# against an F# (the sixth of the key of A). Slides tend to come down out of the note rather than the upward motion we find in the blues.

The tune "Sally Goodin" is equally popular in old-time fiddling as it is in bluegrass, so you'll get twice the payback for half the work. The better you know the melody, the more ideas you'll be able to generate as you build your own version. Don't forget to compare some of the many recordings of the tune to help develop ideas. To get started, refer to the Eck Robertson recording of this tune as the gold standard for old-time fiddlers. He generated a number of variations on the melody that players still quote today.

To cultivate your improvisational skills, it's just as useful to focus on one or two measures to build creative ideas as it is to attempt to solo across the entire tune. For instance, use the backing track to focus on the last two measures of the A section for Sally Goodin as discussed in the opening material on cadences on pages 28 - 29:

CADENCES

Here are two versions of the tune to demonstrate how stylistic and personal touches can be added to help individualize the melody.

Sally Goodin

Sally Goodin

CAJUN

As is the case with old-time and bluegrass, the Cajun fiddle style has evolved over time. When the English ousted five generations of French settlers from Nova Scotia in 1755, many exiled Acadian families were granted land in Louisiana, where their music absorbed new influences, like African, Caribbean, and European.

In the only region in the country at the time where escaped slaves, Native Americans, Spanish and French lived in harmony and intermarried, black Creoles later developed zydeco music. Both Cajun and zydeco music feature the traditional instrumentation of voice, fiddle, accordion and washboard, but as zydeco developed in the 1930s, the style started with traditional instrumentation, then integrated electric bass, guitar and drums. Both styles apply their own brand of the shuffle stroke as defined for old-time and bluegrass, and the rhythm section often places a strong emphasis on the second and fourth beats of the measure. The rhythmic drive of the music makes it difficult to sit still while listening, particularly since the arrangements of many of the tunes include additional sub-rhythms.

We're going to focus on the traditional waltz, "Jolie Blonde," also referred to as "Jol Blon." There are many, many versions of this tune. This one is the result of listening to and combining ideas from several artists.

If on fiddle, the entire tune can be played using the open A and E strings as drones. On viola or cello, you can use the open A string as a drone and play the rest of the melody without double-stops.

The kick-off for the introduction will require short, percussive hits at the frog. This type of introduction is also used by some old-time and bluegrass players.

Consider how each tune you learn shares the same incredible journey your fiddle or violin has taken: it's passed through many hands, minds, and ears to reach the moment you finally adopt it into your life.

Jolie Blonde

 BACKING TRACK

FRANCO-AMERICAN

Fiddle music in New England has been deeply influenced by French fiddlers. The mass migration out of Cape Breton landed more French families in Maine than any other area of New England. It's a little-known fact the French are the second largest ethnic group in that state.

Franco-American fiddlers are often accompanied by piano or accordion, and, like so many styles covered in this book, the emphasis is mostly placed on the second and fourth beats of the measure. Early fiddlers tended to play in two or three keys and held the instrument on their arm, not the shoulder. The music also includes a large number of waltzes, variations on Irish and Scottish tunes, and repertoire imported from Canadian territories such as Montreal and Quebec.

Of particular note is the slur into an accented note. This type of phrase can be found in other styles, as well, so it's worth isolating the technique during practice.

Another important attribute involves the placement of an accenting pattern that pivots:

♦ Place your bow arm at a right angle and rest the bow on your D string.

♦ Start by isolating the upbows on the upbeat. Try to move your bow in a small circle so that you start each accented note in the same place on your bow.

♦ Don't drag the accented note out for its full value: shadow the accent with a subtle airplane liftoff in the shape of a horizontal "V," thinking of the accent as the pointed bottom of the "V" while the subtle lift-off corresponds to the top of the "V."

♦ Now isolate the downbow motion.

♦ Fuse the two and repeat enough times to instill this bowing pattern into muscle memory.

♦ Then add the double stops.

Reel de Remi

🔊 **BACKING TRACK**

Franco-American fiddle music is an audible reflection of mostly self-taught immigrants from French Canada who brought their music with them as my grandfather did. Although bowing patterns between musicians is often quite different, particularly from early recordings, the pulse seems to be the constant. Listen for the call and response phrasing within the tunes that got much of its emphasis from songs sung in kitchens and at house parties.

DON AND CINDY ROY, FRANCO—AMERICAN MUSICIANS FROM MAINE

WESTERN SWING

It don't mean a thing if it…

This upbeat musical style will challenge you to learn how to swing. And improvise.

Swing music heated up in the 1920s with horn-driven big bands performing in large dance halls and became the dominant form of popular music between 1936 and 1946. The style was integrated into fiddle music by a number of western bands since the fiddle had made its journey west in the hands of settlers.

In the early days, Western swing was particularly popular in Texas, California, and Oklahoma, and the fiddle was central to its sound, as it is today. Bandleader, fiddler, mandolinist, singer, and songwriter Bob Wills toured using various combinations of fiddle, piano, vocals, rhythm guitar, tenor banjo, steel guitar, and bass. While there were other Western Swing bands, Wills is the best-known name to represent the genre today. Over his career, he toured with many fiddlers including Johnny Gimble, Jesse Ashlock, Cecil Brower, and Louis Tierney. Fiddlers in Wills' band tapped into a wide range of techniques including the double shuffle, triplets, parallel fifths, and syncopation. Sometimes, he'd tour with two or even three fiddlers who would play double and triple fiddle parts.

Although Wills is known for a number of original tunes, we will focus on the traditional tune, "Beaumont Rag," a tune that's popular among the old-time and bluegrass as well as Western Swing players. Fiddlers in this style play the melody, fillers between lyrics and solos.

It's important to learn how to capture the swing sound. Many players mistakenly default into a staccato execution of dotted eighth notes, but swing is based on a triplet feel. Here are some warm-ups you can practice to train your ears and bow arm.

This first warm-up will support your ability to hear a constant stream of triplets. Warm up on triplets first. Try to emphasize the first of each triplet, then apply less volume to the other two notes. As you develop the ability to alternate between lightly accentuated notes versus inferred pitches, the skill will become extremely useful for many of the styles in this book.

Next, focus on hearing the triplets as you tie the first two together to learn how to differentiate between a swing feel based on a triplet subtext versus falling into a dotted eighth note feel.

Practice the following bowing pattern to master switching bow direction on the "and" of the beat rather than the downbeat. This bow stroke will help generate a swing sound. While improvising, you don't need to use the pattern exclusively. Similar to how we discussed the importance of internalizing the groove essential to old-time fiddling by practicing the shuffle stroke, your goal for Western swing, jazz and Gypsy jazz should be to internalize the swing feel and sound.

Western Swing fiddling is comprised of long bowed melodies, breakdown fiddle tunes and swing solos. Most Western Swing songs begin with a fiddle kick off. These are played in a long-bow style using the middle two thirds of the bow. In general, bow lengths and slurs last for two beats. Tunes such as "Home in San  *Antone," "Old Fashioned Love," "Faded Love," "Maiden's Prayer," and "Right or Wrong" display the slow, even, well-crafted bow strokes played with a light and upbeat feel. In the left hand, listen for the placement of hammer-ons approaching specific notes in the melody. These can vary from a whole step to a minor third below the melody tone. Listen for the timing and length of the hammer-on, as they are longer than grace notes. Tunes like "Take Me Back to Tulsa," "Stay All Night," and "Crippled Turkey" represent the country fiddling style. The bowing patterns will be more fiddle oriented and the slurs may not be as predictable. Listen to the recordings carefully to decipher the bowings. This is how I practice to capture that infectious sound of the style. As far as solos go, I listen to Louis Tierney and Joe Holley for their Joe Venuti influenced jazz solos and Johnny Gimble and Keith Coleman for more sophisticated jazz harmony, horn-like phrasing, and innovative double stops. The most influential Western Swing recordings for me have been Bob Wills and the Texas Playboys' 11-record radio live set "The Tiffany Transcriptions," as well as the most tasteful fiddling by Keith and Johnny on "For the Last Time." As Bob Wills would say "Ahhh haaa!"*

KATIE GLASSMAN, NATIONAL SWING FIDDLE CHAMPION, WESTERN FLYERS

In the B section, the four-bar motif repeats three times. You can replace some of the repetitions or all of them. Here are three classic examples. The entirety of the first idea can be played in a lower or upper octave, or you can shift to a new octave when the idea repeats.

The second and third examples are based on the double shuffle, a string crossing technique popularized by the tune "Orange Blossom Special," but applied in a few old-time and bluegrass tunes long before OBS became a big hit.

When I first started teaching in New York City in the 1970s, I placed an ad in the Village Voice for students and practically every phone call started off with, "Can you teach me how to play the Orange Blossom Special?" It's the three-note shape of the phrase using eighth notes that makes this motif so interesting. We are left with an unfulfilled eighth note in the second half of the second beat that is filled with the first eighth of the repeated three-note phrase. It takes six beats to come back around to the first of the two E's landing on the downbeat again.

Beaumont Rag B Section Variations:

Melody

Variations

Gypsy jazz or jazz Manouche, is a sub-genre of swing music that was first pioneered and made famous by the French guitarist Django Reinhardt and violinist Stephane Grappelli. Together they formed the Quintette du Hot Club of France,

which performed fiery and soulful arrangements of swing classics and original compositions with a French flair. One of the main characteristics of Gypsy jazz is the role of the rhythm guitar, which provides the heartbeat of the groove and emulates a drummer with "la pompe". Today, like most musical genres, Gypsy jazz has taken on a more stylistically inclusive approach and it is not uncommon for modern Gypsy jazz groups to include influences from Latin, classical, funk, contemporary jazz, and Balkan music.

JASON ANICK, BERKLEE PROFESSOR AND INTERNATIONALLY TOURING VIOLINIST

The following transcription of "Beaumont Rag" will provide you with the bare bones melody. Refer back to the examples provided in *How to Generate Variations* on page 26 to develop your own variations. You can also find dozens of versions of this melody to help stimulate ideas for how to make it your own.

Beaumont Rag

BACKING TRACK

A Festival of Violin & Fiddle Styles

AMERICAN POPULAR STYLES

~ Blues

~ Swing

~ Pop/Rock

When it comes to music generated in America, this last century has hosted an explosion of new styles. And the same golden rule applies to blues, swing, jazz, rock, pop, hip hop, funk, etc. as to traditional roots styles: the groove is everything. If you can't strongly define the rhythmic drive for each style without speeding up, slowing down, or understating it, none of the styles you pursue will sound authentic.

The styles in this section require your original musical ideas. If you think you've never improvised before, you're wrong. Your entire life has been an improvisation, including everything you say each day. It isn't necessary to have a single idea in your head. Here are a few simple steps you can take to develop ideas:

♦ Choose one pitch and experiment with different rhythms.

♦ Use varying compliments of horizontal and vertical motion with your bow to develop a vocabulary of articulations for that note. Legato is easiest because gravity invites the bow to stay on the string. Try to develop as many different entrances and exits as you can while working with that one pitch to develop a range between sandy, gruff, guttural with wispy or subtle entrances. Can you create a swell in the middle of the note? At its end? What else can you do to articulate or ornament that single pitch?

♦ Find a second note and rotate back and forth between the two. This is your opportunity to explore rhythmic ideas. Enjoy the silence between the notes just as much as the transitions, articulations, and rhythms you sample.

♦ Create a variation on the melody. Start with just one phrase. Then two. See if you can play a stretch of melody followed by a variation on it and then play freely in the key before you circle back to a quote from the melody, a variation and so on.

The blues is most often performed in a twelve-bar structure:

I7 - I7 - I7 - I7

IV7 - IV7 - I7 - I7

V7 - IV7 - I7 - I7

Translated into the key of G, the key for our blues tune, "Blues at Dawn."

G7 - G7 - G7 - G7

C7 - C7 - G7 - G7

D7 - C7 - G7 - G7

And swing typically uses a thirty-two bar container. A - A - B - A (8 bars per section). The last four bars of the final A section often offer a slight melodic and/or harmonic variation to signifty the end of the form.

> The biggest mistake newbie improvisers make is to think they have to come up with ever-changing ideas. Not true. Repetition is just as useful as inventiveness.

THE BLUES

An intensely emotional style, the blues was developed by African American singers and fiddlers during the days of slavery. This important art form later inspired the development of a group of musical styles regarded as the classic music of America: boogie woogie, ragtime, rhythm and blues, swing, jazz, and rock/pop.

There are several features the blues introduced to American music: the pentatonic (five-note) scale outlined below; the option of a flatted third and/or fifth, called "blue notes," slide technique, improvised solos, and a twelve-bar form.

The country blues includes three chords, while its jazz blues cousin is more harmonically complex. You can ignore the chords in either case and use a pentatonic scale that corresponds with the key signature for the melody (in this case, G) for soloing as a first step toward developing your improvisational skills, but a knowledge of the chords will provide you with the platform for more interesting solos.

Horns tend to prefer keys with flats such as F, Bb, Eb, and Ab; guitarists prefer the keys of E and B; and bowed strings are more accustomed to keys like G, A, D, and C. If you want to be ready for all situations, then practice like jazz musicians, who master the harmonic form for the blues in all twelve keys to get ready to play at jam sessions.

Start by mastering the minor pentatonic scale based on the I (one) chord—in this case, the G7 chord—because "Blues at Dawn" is in the key of G:

Root (G), flatted third (Bb), third (B), fourth (C), flatted fifth (Db), fifth (D), flatted seventh (F♮). Then pursue learning the pentatonic scales for the IV and V chords.

For more information, see my Hal Leonard book, *Rockin' Out with Blues Fiddle* (HL00695612).

I came from a very musical family; they weren't famous or anything. But I had never, ever, been up close to a fiddle or a violin in my life. I'd seen it at a distance and I heard the country white fiddlers play. But, it didn't sound like what I wanted to play. So I just kept plunking on that old bowl-shaped broad-backed mandolin my dad had given me, which we called a "tato-bug." Then, one day I heard this blind man playing

a fiddle. His name was Roland Martin, and he was a half-brother to Carl Martin who played mandolin. Roland played the fiddle and Martin played the bass fiddle. And then nobody, and I mean nobody, played the bass fiddle with a bow. And Martin would play the bass—spinnin' around and sawing on it and making slides, and he had a guy playing the guitar, and I thought that was heaven! And so this blind man was sitting there nodding, and his fiddle was lying on the bed. And it was just drawing me, drawing me, and I just had to touch it. And I plucked on it and I couldn't turn loose. He jumped up, and yelled, "Let that violin alone!" He never called it a fiddle, he called it a violin. And he kind of frightened me, but I was determined to play a fiddle.

I told my daddy, "I got to have a violin." He said, "Well, you know, I got nine kids. There's eleven of us in the family. My pay isn't enough to buy you a fiddle. But I tell you what I'll do, son: You go around the trash piles, in the alleys, and see if you can find an old seasoned-out dirt box. And I did. And the old man came in the evening, from work—he worked til five o'clock at the blast furnace—and he took a pocket knife, cut me out a violin, and carved the neck out and everything, and varnished it with something we called "japalac."

Then one day my father said "Son, look in the doghouse, there's a surprise for you." I looked in the doghouse. You couldn't guess what it was. To me it looked like a miniature coffin, a little black wooden case. He said, "Get it. That's yours!" I brought it out in the light, it was a full-sized violin. And, oh my goodness! I-I-I was thrilled to no end! And I almost never, never, never got home, stopping beside the road, playing for the chipmunks, squirrels, or what—birds—I scared everything, I guess!

And I started from there, Then, other fiddle players, black fiddle players and itinerant ones, come through there. My mother didn't take well to 'em. She was a very religious woman, and she called them rounders, trollops, scalawags. Just pure bums, so to speak. In other words, they were carrying a stick. That's what we black people say when you're down on your luck and don't know or care where you're going, and you're trying to forget where you came from.

I learned from the most notorious fiddle player called Steve Todder. Then, I met other musicians. Guys like Gabe. Long, tall, slim guy. He looked a little bit like Stepin Fetchit. Not in a comical way, but he was an old time fiddle player, out of the Gay Nineties. Gabe, and Henry Alexander. Then later on, that's when I got a little older, I heard Lonnie Johnson, and…oh I can just name a bunch of those black fiddle players that the world never heard of.

HOWARD "LOUIE BLUIE" ARMSTRONG, STRING BAND FIDDLER

Blues at Dawn

by Julie Lyonn Lieberman

🔊 BACKING TRACK

Pretend your bow is a drummer's stick and imagine you can make the most lethargic person in the world get up and dance.

SWING

Swing influenced the development of the field of jazz. Since the inception of swing music in the 1920s and '30s, styles like bebop, cool and modern jazz, and a number of variations such as fusion, and the integration of the Brazilian Bossa Nova have been fused into the jazz scene. The skills you develop for swing, such as mastering the 32-bar structure, generating original ideas, and capturing the groove, will cross-apply to the more complex harmonic structure required to play jazz tunes.

The most popular structure for a swing tune is the same as for a jazz tune: it consists of four eight-bar sections: AABA.

If you haven't tried to play jazz, you might not realize how comprehensive the training is. Certainly, you must cultivate the ability to swing (see "Western Swing" in the *American Roots Styles* section). Other important skills include mastering the use of chromatic motion, dexterity in all twelve keys, a working knowledge of four primary three-part chords and seven primary four-part chords, the memorization of chord progressions in relationship to the melody of any given tune, as well as the ability to improvise over the longer 32-bar form versus the 12-bar form for the blues. Yes, this is a huge undertaking! But, for "Strings du Swing," we'll start with an easier course of action by focusing on some basics.

Take a moment to familiarize yourself with the chromatic scale. Experiment with fingerings but make sure you maintain a light touch so that any finger responsible for playing two consecutive notes can float up a half step without a slide or smear.

It's fine to use alternate names for some of the pitches. Opt for whatever enables you to play in tune and easily summon a picture in your mind regarding where to place each finger.

There are no set rules regarding how to use chromatic motion while soloing, but there are a few guidelines that will provide you with the tools to sound good. To begin, you can apply a chromatic half step below any of the chord tones as a grace note.

You might also want to experiment with moving in half steps to travel between two primary notes.

Early swing tunes often provide the option of soloing using the scale identified by the key signature. For instance, the classic chord progression found in many tunes, called a ii-V7-I progression, can be boiled down to the same scale.

Chord symbols provide essential information regarding how to alter the scale. It's easiest to see this in the key of C, a scale that has no sharps or flats. Notice how the minor symbol informs the player to flat the third and seventh of the ii (two) chord, in this case, D minor. And the dominant seventh (7) symbol informs the player to flat the seventh of the V (five) chord, the G7. These are called *chordal scales* because their pitches have been derived from the chord symbols.

We are going to work on a popular form known as *rhythm changes*. As with the blues, this is a structure that can be applied to any key. All you have to say at a jam session is, "Let's play rhythm changes," or "changes," or even "rhythm," and name the key. The key of B♭ is the most commonly called key for rhythm changes, but my students and I practice the harmonic progressions for rhythm changes as well as the blues in all twelve keys.

The harmonic structure is a spin-off from George Gershwin's song, "I Got Rhythm." The chord changes include a device called a *turnaround*. The relationship between the first four chords, I-VI-ii-V7, can be found three times in the A section of the tune.

Throughout the 1900s, this art form became more complex, and therefore more challenging. Jazz players can't always base their improvisations on one scale for a large number of jazz compositions. They use the key signature for the melody and then base their solos on the notes of each chordal scale as determined by the chord changes. This can sometimes mean changing tonal maps every few beats.

In this case, you can improvise using a B♭ scale and then add a few *Gemini notes*, a term I use to describe a degree of the scale that "changes its mind" to reflect the motion of the chords. For instance, during the third and fourth beats of the first measure, the B♭ in the scale will raise a half step to a B in order to conform to the major third of the key of G since there is a G7 chord in the accompaniment.

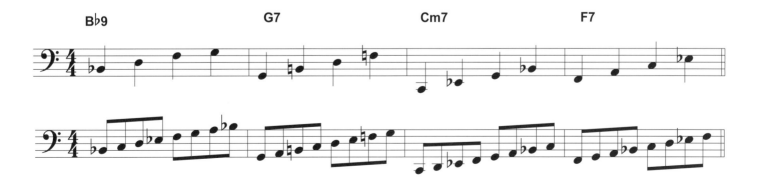

After you've explored soloing in the key of B♭ with a few Gemini notes peppered into the mix, focus on practicing the chord tones for the turnaround to heighten the challenge. Once these additional pathways have been embedded in your ears and muscle memory, you will then be able to access a number of new possibilities while soloing.

Use the backing track to support your ability to hear and feel the four eight-bar phrases contained within this 32-bar form. For improvisation, you can use the scale from the key signature for the tune, "Swingin' the Changes."

Swingin' the Changes

by Julie Lyonn Lieberman

ROCK/POP/FUNK

When the blues went electric in the 1950s, the style was renamed *Rhythm and Blues*. Due to racial discrimination, the Billboard charts listed African American artists under "R&B," and placed white artists under the label "rock." Yet, early rock artists stole most of their sound and even whole songs as well as arrangements and stage moves from black artists. Eventually, the rock category spawned hundreds of new forms, from heavy metal to Gothic rock to pop music and the Billboard charts became more integrated.

Today's solid-body instruments for bowed strings are often outfitted with five, six and even seven strings, so the differences among the instruments of the traditional string quartet have blurred. Octave strings or a special effect called a *harmonizer* enable violinists and violists to thicken their sound and add an octave below bowed pitch, which provides players with an option to generate bass lines using pizzicato when not playing the melody or soloing.

Many rock artists, when using a string section, hire an arranger who writes classical background lines for the string section. However, to truly sound like a rock violinist, violist or cellist, you'll require a different set of skills from reading scores written for classical players. These skills include the ability to create a riff, to use your bow rhythmically when not playing the melody or soloing, and most importantly, mastery over expressive techniques without relying solely on sweeping bows and vibrato.

Pentatonic Scales and Patterns

There are two types of pentatonic scale: major and minor. If this is a style you wish to pursue, then these two scales will become the backbone of your tool kit while playing with bands. The examples are in the key of E, because that's a popular key for guitarists.

Major: 1-2-3-5-6-8

Minor: 1-♭3-4-5-♭7-8

Singers choose keys based on their vocal range. They aren't going to ask you to name the keys you feel comfortable with. You could end up playing in D♭ or F♯ if that's the key the lead singer feels most comfortable with. For that reason, my rock students make it a point to master their pentatonic scales in all twelve keys and apply patterns to the notes, so they aren't locked into a limited pathway on the instrument.

It's useful to practice patterns as a preparatory step toward improvisation. Here's an example:

Depending on the taste of whoever leads the band, the string player may need to play an introduction to the song, fillers between lyrics, a solo, some pads or rhythmic comping, and maybe even generate a line to end the piece.

Pads, Comping, and Fillers

The rhythm section, usually comprised of guitar, bass, and keyboard, supports the singer. Most vocalists will not opt for an instrumental solo behind them while singing the lyrics to a song lest the words are obscured. If they do invite you to play, it's better to play long tones, known as *pads*, or a simple, repetitive rhythmic idea that supports but doesn't compete with what they're singing, often referred to as *comping*. Here are a few examples in the key of E.

Melody

Examples

How to Invent an Introduction or Ending

Once you know the key the song is in, you can either echo a melodic line from the song or create new ideas for your introduction or ending, or both. If you're playing an introduction, try not to resolve your phrase to the root note of the key. Try to ask a musical question so that your introduction acts like a magnet for the opening lyrics of the song. The length of the introduction and/or ending can be determined by the leader of the band. Here's an abbreviated example based on the opening melody outlined above:

It's certainly acceptable to end the song with a similar musical line to whatever you played for your introduction, but this time, end on the tonic (the root note of the key).

Vibrato is a personal choice in this idiom. If you decide to play with a band, demonstrate how you would sound with and without vibrato so the group can make a decision that complements the band's overall sound. Special effects using a stomp box present another topic for discussion by the members of the band. For example, if it's a folk/rock band, special effects may not be as appropriate as they are with a heavy metal band.

STYLIZED VIBRATO

All About Riffs

Have you ever wondered why Pachelbel's Canon is performed SO many times even though it was composed in the 1680s? Or how novelists can condense an entire book into a few captivating lines for promotion? Whether you call it a riff, an ostinato, a loop, or a musical phrase, the ability to create a short, repeating melodic line coupled with a catchy rhythmic idea could earn you a million dollars and certainly has done just that for a number of musicians.

Your ability to build a tasty riff will enable you to work well with a looper, create catchy backing lines, or even compose longer melodies. That's because a riff is to composition what a Haiku poem is to writing. It encapsulates the essence of a juicy idea. There's a clear beginning, middle and end in a short space of time, yet the idea begs to be repeated.

A riff can serve as an introduction to a song, an accompaniment, or as the central theme for an entire piece of music. And we can find examples of this musical device throughout a number of styles. For instance, the Griot singers of West Africa accompany themselves on the Kora with highly repetitive and captivating figures. In fact, a number of instruments and styles throughout Africa use highly repetitious lines, sometimes interlocking several simultaneously like the inner workings of a watch. Ethnomusicologists have referred to this as *hocket technique*. We can also find riffs in Afro-Cuban music, Kansas City jazz, the blues, and Baroque music dating back to the thirteenth century. It was also good enough for Maurice Ravel in his composition, "Bolero."

Yet, it's surprisingly difficult to come up with a catchy idea that leaves us hungering for more of the same. While teaching an online university course to string teachers interested in alternative styles, we did a unit on this topic. They listened to a number of classic riffs from all over the world and their assignment that week was to come up with a two-bar riff. None of them were able to accomplish this. At the end of the week, I received a series of lovely linear melodies or short ideas that ended on the tonic.

So, how do you get started?

Choose a key you feel comfortable with. Limit yourself to a handful of pitches and two measures to begin with. Try to avoid using sequential quarter notes because a walking rhythm can weigh down the melody and make it sound like a march. Syncopation can help contribute tension to the phrase. So can slices of silence.

Just for the fun of it, I've extracted melodic quotes from tunes in this book and turned them into riffs. Admittedly, these probably won't earn me a million dollars, and these examples could just as easily fit into our opening material under how to create variations on a melody, but this will give you a running start. Let's see if you can figure which melodies I extracted the lines from.

For riffs from around the world, see my Hal Leonard book, *Twelve-Key Practice: The Path to Mastery and Individuality (HL00286780)*.

A Few Classic Riffs

Jimi Hendrix, Purple Haze
George Thorogood, Bad to the Bone
Ritchie Blackmore, Smoke on the Water
Cream, Sunshine of Your Love
Rolling Stones, Satisfaction
Bobby McFerrin, Grace

This is our time, in the 21st century to broaden our mission and vision. Expand your palate to embrace and learn from the diversity in music. Rock on!

MARK WOOD,
EMMY AWARD WINNING COMPOSER AND
INNOVATOR, ELECTRIC STRINGS

Rock, Pop, Funk, Rap... What's the Difference?

Every style of music includes its own rhythmic identity. Within the pop field, this is also true. It's all about the groove. Whether we're talking about rock, pop, funk, rap, hip hop, or R&B, the band will always include a trap set for the drummer and possibly hand percussion. The bass player will lock into the drummer's groove, as will other members of the rhythm section, like the keyboardist and guitarist. Fortunately, these styles tend to all be in 4/4.

For a moment, pretend your cranium is made up of muscles. Then imagine your ears have been gifted sets of muscles, similar to how your upper arm hosts the deltoid, the triceps and the biceps muscles. One aural "muscle" for melody, one for harmony, one for chords, and one for rhythm. Which muscle do you suppose you use the most every day when you practice? Yup. The melody muscle. If you haven't caught on by now, all the styles covered in this book will require super-boosting your rhythmic muscle.

I love making up words, so here goes... *quadriplex listening.* First, it's best to focus on one instrument at a time to understand and include aspects of their role in the band into your musicianship. Strengthening your "rhythm muscle" will require learning how to focus your ears—exclusively, to begin with—on the drummer. Then the bass player, followed by the guitarist or keyboardist, and finally, the vocalist. You can certainly play around with the order, but eventually your goal will be to hear all the instruments equally and simultaneously. Then you can weave between melodic and rhythmic ideas at will while arranging your part(s) and/or soloing.

Here are a few essential questions you can use to identify within each song:

♦ Does the rhythm section accentuate the first and third beats or the second and fourth?

♦ Is there an eighth, quarter, or triplet rhythmic subtext? Or a combination?

♦ Where do the accents fall within the phrase?

◆ Is there a rhythmic idea that keeps repeating? Sometimes the answer will come from a member of the rhythm section other than the drummer. You can either lock into that instrument's rhythmic pattern or play a repetitive contrasting rhythmic idea. Can you figure out which popular funk song this pattern comes from?

In order to play popular styles, you will be compelled to reevaluate the way you've been taught because you will need to use a different part of your brain. You will no longer just read notes off of paper with expressive markings. You will learn how to create on the spot, because playing rock, blues, swing or jazz will call on you to experiment and create extemporaneously. Through that process, you will figure out the sounds you personally like and overcome the belief that anything that comes out of you has to be perfect. It's a journey of self-acceptance. Of learning to allow yourself to experiment. Improvisation and rocking out has healing powers.

JOE DENINZON, ROCK AND JAZZ VIOLINIST

CELTIC STYLES

~ One Tune, Many Versions

~ Irish

~ Scottish

~ Shetland Islands

~ Cape Breton

INTRODUCTION TO CELTIC FIDDLING

The repertoire of Celtic music is vast, with numerous versions of each tune. Some historians trace Celtic fiddling back to the 1600s, while others date the art back to the 1200s. Yet, the word "fidl" shows up in a fourth-century poem. Today, when we use the term "Celtic" we're referring to areas like Ireland, Scotland, the Isle of Man (between Ireland and England), and Brittany (in France). The Celts, also known as the Gauls, traveled throughout Western Europe in earlier times. So, why is any of this information relevant to us today?

There are a few important takeaways:

1. Depending on where the Celts settled, their music was incorporated into the region, and/or they incorporated ideas from local musicians.

2. Fiddle tunes and techniques were taught by ear and each region had its own repertoire. Sometimes, tunes even differed village to village in countries like Ireland, Scotland, England, and the Shetland Islands, long before fiddlers migrated to areas like Cape Breton, New England, and Appalachia.

3. Earlier in the book, I mentioned how versions of tunes are only as faithful as the technique, memory and imagination of the player. Passed from generation to generation by ear, only the recording industry in the 1900s and the eventual notation of a percentage of these tunes has served to lock in specific versions of each tune. But even so, we can find enormous differences among players of the same tune.

The tricky terrain called "traditional" lures us into thinking we must be faithful to the exact version of a tune we learn from an authentic Irish, Scottish, Cape Breton, or Shetland Islands. But years ago, I ran a test for my Hal Leonard book, *Planet Musician*. A student helped me collect renditions of the same tune from five famous Irish fiddlers. Each of them insisted their version—melody, ornamentation and bowings—was the only correct way to play the tune.

When you listen to and learn a number of tunes, you will be able to detect snippets of familiar melodic phrases and patterns within the enormous body of Celtic-oriented repertoire, and some fiddlers play the same melody as a reel and then flip it into a jig, depending on the dance steps they accompany. But ultimately, it's the bow patterns and individualized twists and turns each performer adds to their repertoire that helps individualize each tune when performed.

I've searched for popular tunes to prepare you for jam sessions. Some of those tunes have been adapted into old-time fiddling and even bluegrass repertoire.

Celtic tunes from Ireland, like fiddle tunes from almost everywhere in the world, were mostly used to accompany dancers. The common tune forms include reels, jigs, slip jigs, marches, and slow airs. Once you acquaint yourself with each type of tune, it becomes easier to learn new tunes. You'll be able to quickly grasp the meter, the cadence of the music, and appropriate ornamentation you can add.

Ornamentation

Let's get started with ornaments common to most Celtic tunes. A number of these ornaments are related to the bagpipes, an instrument found throughout these territories. When new to adding ornamentation to the melody, don't make the mistake of automatically allowing your bow arm to accentuate the grace note rather than the primary pitch it leads to, unless specified by the style. To be prepared, practice both ways: lean into your right index finger to accentuate the ornament, then lighten pressure for the grace note and lean in on the primary pitch. Restated, each ornament calls for a particular participation from the bow, so make sure to listen to recorded examples.

The following ornaments can be modified according to taste and style and there are no set rules regarding when to add an ornament. Your personal taste will dictate the choices you make. But in general, listen for and think about the arc of each musical phrase, and ornament notes you wish to highlight.

The "Irish triplet," also known as a "bowed treble," is a popular bow technique. If it is notated, it's usually shown as a triplet, but it's bowed as two sixteenth notes followed by an eighth or even tighter: two thirty-second notes followed by a dotted eighth. It's up to the player when and where to place this ornament, though generally it's only added to chosen quarter notes within the melody. Some players bow it lightly, while others dig into the string. There's also disagreement pertaining to bow direction. Some players only apply the bowed treble on the downbow. I advocate mastering the bowing on an upbow as well so that you're prepared for all eventualities.

Left-hand ornaments include grace notes, mordents and turns. The grace note is played quickly and lightly from a neighboring scale tone.

The mordent adds a quick dip under and back to the primary pitch.

Some players give more emphasis to the first note of the turn, while others emphasize the final note. The speed can vary, as well, though the entire figure must fit into a beat unless indicated otherwise.

These are the most popular ornaments, but there are additional variants depending on the player and point of origin. As stressed above, it's important to listen to authentic players to expand your vocabulary of possibilities.

Is One Source Enough?

I'm sometimes limited to downloading or purchasing a printed copy of a tune if the audio isn't available on YouTube or iTunes, but I prefer to learn tunes by ear. There are websites that allow me to paste the Youtube URL into their mp3 converter so I can use a software program to slow it down to study all the subtle nuances within the melody. Then, I search for as many versions of the tune as I can find. This helps me determine the difference between individual interpretation and traditional foundation.

Let's practice this learning approach by examining a couple of measures together. There are so many ideas you can gain by analyzing other fiddlers' choices. Remember how we practiced extracting the harmonic building blocks from a couple of measures in the opening material? Compare the building blocks for measures six and seven in this first staff with the variations. This will help you learn the tune, but more importantly, it will help you configure your own ideas on this or any tune you choose.

The Shetland Fiddler

(two-bar excerpt)

Bare bones melody, measures 6-7:

Three variations:

ONE TUNE...MANY VERSIONS

Since you can purchase dozens of books filled with Celtic fiddle tunes, I've decided to offer a different entrance into this expansive genre. To get started, we will focus on a tune titled "The Shetland Fiddler," also known as "The Hawk" in some circles. Versions of this tune can be traced to the Shetland Islands, Scotland, Ireland, and Cape Breton. Each rendition will help you develop a deeper sense of the differences and similarities among the playing styles.

I am going to present this as a study in variations and options, rather than styles specific to each region, which we'll discuss later in this section. You have two options for how to work with these versions: you can play through them back-to-back or choose a particular passage and cross-compare. You can apply the approach we just explored in "Is One Source Enough?" by extracting the seminal pitches from one or two measures to more fully understand how each version of the tune dances around those pitches.

The Shetland Fiddler aka The Hawk: #1

The Shetland Fiddler aka The Hawk: #2

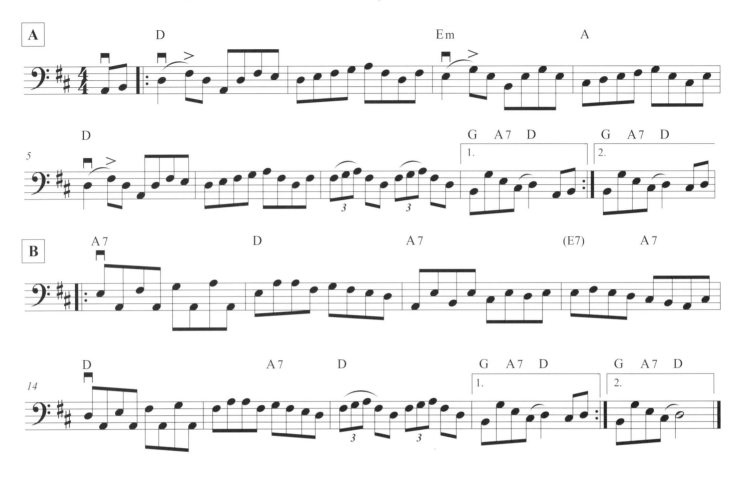

The Shetland Fiddler aka The Hawk: #3

The Hawk aka The Shetland Fiddler: #4

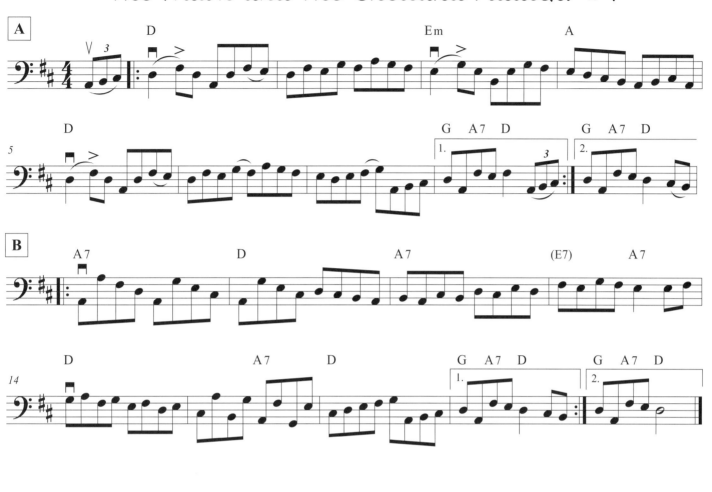

The Hawk aka The Shetland Fiddler: #5

IRISH

All of the ornamentation covered earlier can be tapped into for any Irish tunes you opt to learn. I chose this tune "Drowsy Maggie," to share because it's a popular tune and introduces a few important techniques. The string-crossing pattern comes up in a number of tunes in this genre. Make sure to hover your right elbow over the E note to provide an opportunity to drop your elbow into gravity to highlight the string crossing. Use gravity to whip your bow arm to hit each note in the upper, moving line, so that the pitches on the upper string pop out.

A number of Irish tunes include a line that requires hopping the same finger back and forth across two strings. In this case, the finger that plays the opening E has to also cover the B note that follows. Some players end up distorting their left hand position to reach both notes quickly, but this can invite poor intonation and discomfort in the hand. The solution? Place your finger on both notes simultaneously as if you're about to play a double-stop—or if your finger is too thin, lightly straddle halfway between the two pitches and lift slightly to hop back and forth.

If possible, leave the finger in place while you play the upper D in the third beat of "Drowsy Maggie" so you can easily return to the E and B at the end of the measure. That way, your finger will be ready and waiting rather than hovering above the strings. This finger choreography will leave you free to focus on your right-hand motion between the two strings.

Drowsy Maggie

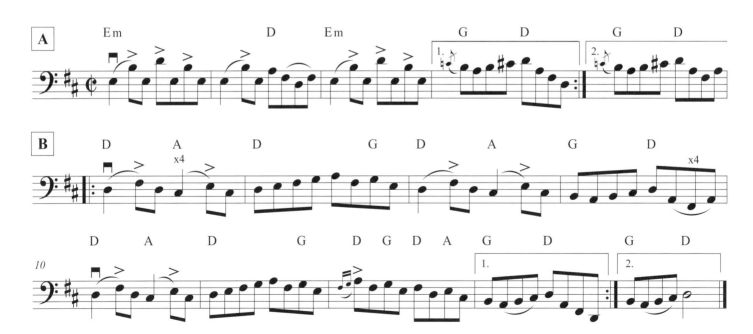

SCOTTISH

Scottish and Irish fiddling share some traits, like the AABB structure and the use of fiddle tunes to accompany dance. They are also dissimilar in many respects. For instance, unlike the aural tradition found in Ireland, many Scottish fiddle tunes have known authors. Henry Playford published the first full collection of Scottish fiddle tunes in 1700. While not all tunes can be credited, composers like Niel Gow (1727-1807), William Marshall (1748-1833), Robert Mackintosh (1745-1807) and James Scott Skinner (1843-1927) were all prominent composers for the fiddle. For this reason, performances of Scottish tunes tend to be more faithful to the original versions, with only the improvised use of ornaments to differentiate individual choices among players. Another difference between Scottish and Irish fiddling is the dotted eighth followed by a sixteenth and/or the sixteenth followed by a dotted eighth, found in the Scottish strathspey.

The Scottish snap takes this one step further by double-dotting the eighth and coupling it with a thirty-second note.

Its opposite, the dotted eighth coupled with a sixteenth is played with more of a triplet feel.

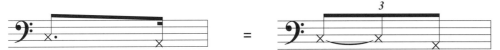

Scottish fiddling tends to include more coloration from the bow than Irish. For instance, entire passages are sometimes played with a staccato bow just short of the flying spiccato found in classical technique.

As mentioned earlier in the introduction, the notated triplets are played more like two sixteenths followed by an eighth note rather than as symmetrical triplets. Scottish fiddlers refer to this as a *birl* or a *cut*. This ornament is also found in Irish fiddling, and is referred to as an *Irish triplet* or *bowed treble*.

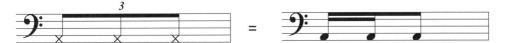

Fiddlers tend to choose bowings as they play. A common bow pattern used in a number of tunes involves slurring across three eighth notes, usually from the upbeat into the next beat. This can occur in the middle of the measure or across two measures:

"Laird o' Drumblair" is a popular Scottish tune and credited as one of Scott Skinner's best-known tunes.

The label "Scottish fiddling" arches like an umbrella over a number of smaller regional styles. While they all make use of certain key stylistic attributes, such as incorporating a gentle swing to their reel and jig rhythms, they are all influenced to various degrees

by the great Highland bagpipes, Gaelic song, Scottish traditional dance, and classical violin playing. The best known of the regional styles are West Highland, Northeast, and the Shetland styles. The West Highland style takes a lot of its modality, melodic contour, and ornamental cues from the bagpipes, while Gaelic song influences the interpretation of slower airs. Reflective of the Highland dancing for which it can be played, the West Highland style tends to be a more aggressive style. The Northeast style blends the bagpipe's ornamental influence with more classical left- and right-hand violin techniques. The Northeast style of playing reflects the needs of country dancing (similar to square dancing) for which it is routinely used. The Shetland style of playing has less bagpipe influence. Instead, it honors its Scandinavian past with the frequent use of "ringing strings," a technique which imitates the Hardanger fiddle of Norway.

MELINDA CRAWFORD PERTU, U.S. NATIONAL SCOTTISH FIDDLING CHAMPION

A Festival of Violin & Fiddle Styles

SHETLAND ISLANDS

The traditional music of the Shetland Islands has certainly been influenced by Irish, English, and Scottish fiddling, as well as Norwegian. In turn, tunes from the Shetland Islands are played in those countries with regional bowings and ornaments. Shetland music is strongly fiddle-based, with the addition of piano, accordion, and/or guitar for accompaniment. Shetland musicians, from traditional fiddler Aly Bain to the more contemporary group, Fiddlers' Bid, regularly tour worldwide.

The first time I heard Aly Bain perform was at the Fox Hollow Folk Festival. His workshop was on the other side of the property, and I somehow got lost and ended up walking through a small wooded area, where his bell-like tones were amplified by the trees. Aly's dexterous string crossing sounded as if his fiddle had only one, long string.

There isn't a tradition of improvisation in Shetland fiddling, but each fiddler develops their own version of the tunes they perform. The bowings add enormous spice to the sound. Particularly the slur into an accented pitch, how accents fall within the melody line, as well as the interplay of stacatto notes that stop short of their time value. Play the bare bones version first:

Aandowin' At Da Bow

Now, compare to how Aly Bain plays "Aandowin' at da Bow."

Aandowin' at da Bow

🔊 **BACKING TRACK**

The fiddle music of Shetland is quite unique. Not only was the fiddle the only instrument used for dancing, but it also had a significant ceremonial role to play in everyday life. The early influences were Norse. The fiddle was used to lead the procession at weddings and funerals. There were tunes for every kind of work including mill tunes, spinning tunes and tunes learned from the "Trows" (Shetlands trolls) which, once heard, could never be forgotten. There was even a tune to play the bride to bed. The use of various tunings are also unique to Shetland…again from our Norse heritage. The passing of time has brought new influences from mainland Scotland and Ireland and the music is now more popular than ever. The music is alive and well today…as it should be.

ALY BAIN, MASTER SHETLAND ISLAND FIDDLER

CAPE BRETON

The music of Cape Breton, located in Nova Scotia, was imported from Scotland by immigrants in the early 1700s. Piano replaced pump organ as accompaniment to the fiddle. There is a powerful walking pulse, often supported by the heel of the player landing on the floor to accentuate the downbeat, particularly when playing strathspeys, but the upstroke is just as powerful as the down. The repertoire includes jigs, reels, marches, strathspeys, hornpipes, and slow airs.

Ornamentation includes the Irish bowed treble, which is referred to as a *cut*, the use of drone strings, and an ornament called a *warble*, that emulates the cut by lightly bouncing a left-hand finger in quick succession. Players also use an effect they call doubling. This technique—referred to as a unison in old-time fiddling—is created by playing a double-stop that uses the pinkie to double the pitch of next highest open string.

I have included two versions of a popular Cape Breton strathspey, "King George IV."

King George IV

This second version of "King George IV" is notated according to Andrea Beaton's approach to performing the tune and will provide you with an example of how each individual artist can make the tune his or her own. The "W" above certain pitches indicates the *warble* described above. Sometimes these are played so quickly that the lower note gets lost or muted, and the finger that plays the higher note ends up being more of a wiggle.

Andrea also uses a double grace note. She plays the pitch above the melody note first, and then graces the melody note with that same upper partner. So for a C# melody note, she would play the D, C#, D, C#, and give the C# a little more value than the D graces.

King George IV

The Cape Breton fiddle style, like most languages, has several dialects. It is a very oral tradition, passed down through families and neighbors. The Cape Breton fiddle style has a very heavy backbeat which is complemented by the accompanying instruments, mainly piano and guitar. The back and forth bowing, which some have called "sawing", is one of the things that differs Cape Breton from other styles. We do less slurry bows and tend to play our strathspeys faster and our reels slower than other styles. This is to accommodate Cape Breton step dancing, a percussive dance style that is very close to the floor. The fiddle style has been highly influenced by bagpipes and the Gaelic language. There are different types of grace notes, cuts, how we pull into the notes rather than just land directly on them that mimic the sounds of the songs or pipes. Each fiddler tends to decorate the tunes in their own way to make it their own.

ANDREA BEATON, CAPE BRETON FIDDLER

EASTERN EUROPEAN STYLES

~ Hungarian

~ Ukrainian

~ Klezmer

~ Roma

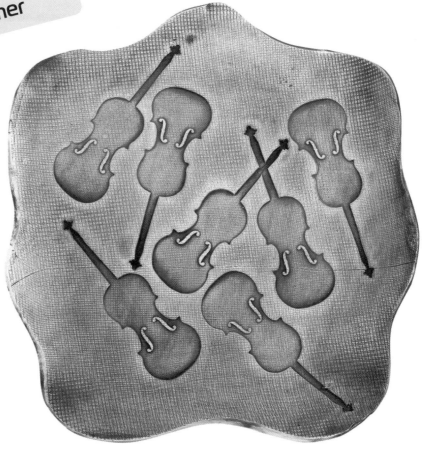

There are a number of robust fiddle styles from Eastern Europe that feature intensely driving rhythms and passionately expressive ballads. The best-known genres are Roma and Klezmer. However, each country in Eastern Europe has developed its own body of fiddle literature. The tunes cover a wide range of forms, often meant to accompany dances like mazurkas, polkas, kolomyjkas, freylekhs, horas, csárdás, legenyes, sîrbas, rucenitsas, to kopanitsas, and more. As is the case with all the styles covered in *A Festival of Violin & Fiddle Styles,* this section will provide a sampling of handpicked tunes chosen to provide you with an overview of some of the styles from this area.

Playing techniques shared across Eastern Europe include a quarter-tone or half-step trill, odd and alternating meter, scales with a gap of a minor third, and left-hand pizzicato, to name a few. There are steep tempo changes across a number of styles. Tunes can easily swivel from major to minor and back again...or vice versa. Some tunes require a good deal of shifting up and down the fingerboard as well as tremendous speed and agility from the bow arm. String players imitate bird sounds, display a wide variety of types of vibrato, apply spiccato and flying spiccato bowings, harmonics, as well as glissandi that are varied in length and speed. Of all the styles covered in this book, the music of Hungary—and Romania in particular—utilize the instrument's capabilities equal to Western canon.

Structurally, the tunes tend to be longer than many of the styles we've covered so far; the length of each section doesn't adhere to four- or eight-bar phrases like so many other fiddle styles. The tonal center can shift, as can the type of scale. Some tunes feature a note or notes that change identities as the tune progresses: first sharped, then flatted, or the other way around.

Among the Roma and klezmer ensembles, the violinist is the "primas:" the soloist and leader of the band. Both groups in Eastern Europe look upon the violin as the instrument—when sounded out—as having the closest sonority to the human voice. Both cultures value the human voice as "God-given." It is believed that the voice was given to humans by this awesome power and so when we sing to him/her we are using the very instrument provided us to praise as well as cry. Thus, the violin became the instrument to best replicate the human voice. My friend and klezmer teacher Leopold Kozlowski (Krakow) once said "Yitskhok, when you draw the bow across your strings you are never playing the violin but instead you are praying." This has stayed with me my entire life, as the violin for me is a vessel that allows me to give pleasure and gratitude to the "power-force" that is greater than me, that created the universe.

YALE STROM, KLEZMER FIDDLER AND COMPOSER, FILMMAKER, AUTHOR

HUNGARIAN

I learned "Kettős Jártatója from Gyimes" from Beth Bahia Cohen. You will enjoy the unique quality of this tune.

The tune alternates between two pitch maps, or scale fragments as Beth calls them, that include G A B C# D and G A B♭ C# D

The G chord frames the melody and the trill should be a quarter-tone trill. I call this type of trill a **vibratrill**. This is a Julieism to describe how you can use a motion akin to vibrato to achieve its sound. But in order to actualize its flutter-like quality, as opposed to the symmetrical nature of classical vibrato, I piggyback the trilling finger on the fingernail of the finger designated to play the lower pitch. In this instance, the finger that plays the C# performs a fast-tempo but brief roll while the trilling finger is actually passive. It comes along for the ride as it "pecks" the string. I'm sure there are other ways to achieve this sound, but that's what works best for me.

When performed in its traditional setting, the ütőgardon plays a rhythmic pattern to accompany the melody. This can be imitated by hitting the strings with the wooden part of the bow. The pluck is created with a left-handed pizzicato.

The music of Gyimes features the violin (hegedű) accompanied by a percussion drone instrument called the ütőgardon, which has three or four gut strings all tuned to D and played by alternating between a snap pizzicato and hitting the strings with a stick. Because the music is mostly dance music, the ütőgardon plays the rhythm of the specific dances. The music of Gyimes comes from villages in the Gyimes Valley located in the eastern Carpathian mountains in Transylvania. Besides regular vibrato, the vibrato trill is also used.

BETH BAHIA COHEN, BERKLEE COLLEGE OF MUSIC, WORLD STRINGS

Kettős Jártatója from Gyimes

A Festival of Violin & Fiddle Styles

UKRAINIAN

Here's a popular Ukrainian tune I picked up from Yale Strom. It's one of my favorite tunes. "Kolomeyke" is a Ruthenian melody. The Ruthenians, also referred to as "Rus" or "Rusyns" are related to the Ukrainians but they have their own language. Their distant relatives can be found in Russia, Lithuania, and other regions of Eastern Europe.

Kolomeyke

KLEZMER

Klezmer fiddle music, though related to genres throughout Eastern Europe, is the music of the Jews. As such, it is heavily influenced by an art form known as *nigun*, sung Jewish religious tunes or melodies that combine lyrics with vocables—sounds that have no meaning, like "Yai-Yai-Yai," yet impart deep emotion. The best-known melodies were transported throughout Eastern Europe and sung in synagogues or used to accompany dance forms such as circle dances like the Bulgar, Freylekhs, Khosisl, or Hora.

Of particular note is the *Doina*, an opportunity for the instrumentalists in the band to solo by embellishing the melody over sustained chords played by the other musicians. Another important feature prevalent in many tunes is the gap of a minor third between two scale tones. This can be found between the second and third tones of the scale in the *Ahava Raba* mode used in the A section of "Der Heyser Bulgar," and between the flatted third and raised fourth in the *Misheberakh* mode.

As is the case with so many styles, the notation can only communicate a limited version of the actual sound. Visually speaking, it would be far too crowded to add all the slides and bends or all those subtle ornaments that defy notation. Keep in mind the violin is imitating the human voice, so try singing the melody with angst yet also a passion for life.

Ahava Raba

Misheberakh Mode

Der Heyser Bulgar

BACKING TRACK

ROMA

The Romany people, also known as Romani, were nicknamed "Gypsies" in the 15th century because it was believed they were from Egypt, but they actually migrated out of Northern India roughly 1,500 years ago. The Roma consider the name "Gypsy," (sometimes spelled Gipsy) an offensive racial slur. A people without a home, they traveled in bands throughout Eastern Europe picking up yet other names, such as "gitan," "Gitano," and "tzigane," among others. Some splinter groups settled in the Middle East, while others traveled to Spain. Later, groups moved through areas of Western Europe, South America and the United States.

Roma have acted as collectors of tunes, picking up modes and repertoire everywhere they've traveled while also impacting the music of each area. Jews and Roma were persecuted in Eastern Europe and often shared violin techniques and repertoire as well as gigs.

There is no such thing as a single Roma style of music; think of the range covered by Flamenco, the Gypsy jazz of Django Reinhardt, the Romanian hard jazz/rock of Ivo Popozov, the raw village music of Taraf de Haiduks, the smooth schmaltz of the Hungarian Gypsy orchestras. There is also a style of music played only by the Roma for themselves, largely vocal and percussive and highly improvised.

What is common to all is their great aptitude as musicians, adopting a professional attitude, learning the local repertoire and generally improving on the performance of the natives through virtuosity, improvisation and showmanship. As periodic travelers, Roma have been an important force in musical cross-pollination; in addition to having command of the local repertoire. They almost certainly have a wide knowledge of music from other regions and countries, and can introduce techniques and flavors which seem mysterious and exotic.

CHRIS HAIGH, FIDDLE PLAYER AND WRITER

Romany music is known for its changes in tempo and extemporaneous ornamented fillers that move at lightning speed. Both are more difficult than one would think. For changes in tempo, you must learn to broadcast the imminent change whether you are about to slow down or speed up. As with the various length slides, the fillers are a part of the ornamentation of the melody and are akin to mini-cadenzas. They are up to the player to generate and often swirl through arpeggiating tones across several octaves, if not more.

Yale Strom collected and transcribed "Song of Ulok" from the Roma of the Carpathian area of Ukraine, though it is possibly Hungarian in origin. When you play the melody, you can take advantage of the held notes to superimpose your own ideas, ranging from extremely simple add-ons to longer flourishes.

The following example is based on measures five and six. Bow as is comfortable to you. Feel free to add slurs.

Melodic Excerpt

Variation

Here's a far more elaborate version of the same two-measure line:

You can also generate interesting ideas that connect two phrases. For instance, in measures fifteen and sixteen, I've added a flourish to connect two ideas.

In order to fit the new material, I cheated the first note of its extra half beat and sixteenth note repetition. I also took advantage of the pause and lengthened it before the new, sixteenth note run. For the last note in the second measure, you could use the same finger that plays the E to slide all the way up your string to reach that D. There's no rush as long as you time the slide to create suspense. When the audience knows where you're headed, you can fit quite a lot into the melody. The trick is to take your time, hear where you're going in your inner ear, and milk it for all it's worth!

Melodic Excerpt

Variation

Song of Ulok

A Festival of Violin & Fiddle Styles

Jazz violinist Eddie South might play "Hejri Kati" which was his theme, a very lovely violin piece, or he'd play a Gypsy air or a czardas or something like that.

He might play a blues, he might play one of the pop tunes of the day, and he had made transcriptions of several classical pieces, which sometimes he played in tempo. He didn't even play it as a classical piece.

And so it was a fascinating job, I mean, because he worked me to death, I mean he really put me in the woodshed to try to learn those piano parts. Especially the Gypsy pieces, because the piano parts he had seemed to be transcriptions of what the cimbalom players did. And so the page would be black with notes. I'm running all up and down—arpeggios all over the place. And he's playing these long lines beautifully, and I mean I'm saying, "Yeah, okay. Thanks a lot."

But that worked. I mean it really was the context.

Eddie South played those Gypsy melodies so authentically, that the King of the Gypsies used to come and hear us. And he'd come in with all of his entourage and everything, and they'd sit there and cry…Eddie would play all these things and they'd cry. And Eddie'd invite them down, they'd have champagne, and they'd tell him what a great artist he was, and that he was a black Gypsy. They really loved him, and they paid such homage to him wherever he worked. I mean he would get telegrams, he would get flowers. I remember one time someone called him long distance and asked him to play something for them over the phone. And so he was on the phone, playing unaccompanied whatever this melody was. The people who respected him really loved his artistry. He was a remarkable musician.

– DR. BILLY TAYLOR, JAZZ PIANIST, CBS SUNDAY MORNING NEWS JAZZ HOST. 1988 INTERVIEW, JULIE'S NPR SERIES "THE TALKING VIOLIN"

"Hora Dreapta" can be played against a C drone for the most part, with a steady eighth note rhythmic pulse. There is a short stint against a G drone measures 29-33 and again, measures 66-69. An A drone accompanies the remainder of the tune, from measures 70-91. This tune is thought to have come from Romania.

Hora Dreaptă

Hora Dreaptă (continued)

In 1965, I was born into a family of Gypsy violinists descended from Janos

Bihari, known as the "King of the Gypsy Violinists." From early childhood, I was surrounded by music. When I was five, my father took me to the best violin player in Budapest, who taught me classical violin technique and ornamentation.

As a very young boy, I started playing in my uncle Sandor's and father Antal's band and performed as the first violin of a Gypsy Orchestra by the age of nine.

Later, I studied classical violin at the Béla Bartók Conservatory of Budapest, where I won first prize for classical violin in 1984.

Belgium was my musical home between 1986 and 1996. I performed with my ensemble quite often at Les Atéliers de la Grande Ile club in Brussels. Today, I usually perform with an ensemble composed of virtuoso musicians as well as classical musical educators who are also well-versed in the folklore traditions of the Hungarian Gypsies.

I combine jazz, classical, Gypsy (Romani), and even swing techniques in the style of Django Reinhardt and Stephane Grappelli into my compositions and performances. My repertoire is pretty unconventional. It's a mix of different styles from the Balkans and Russia, but first and foremost I play Gypsy music.

It's almost impossible to describe my music in few words. Once, a journalist asked me to explain, but after the concert, he answered his question: "It's unorthodox gypsy fusion music." I think this pretty much describes my style. For me, music comes from God. I have made a new style of music. Jazz is like Gypsy music, so it gives liberty and freedom. I've changed many elements of the Gypsy style and play my music with constant rhythm, colors and moods changes.

I think my music reaches a wider audience because I have performed for many people who have differing musical tastes. Young people like the jazz in my music, older audience maybe the classical influences or my special pizzicato. There is something for everyone, so I think the future of this music is incredibly exciting.

ROBY LAKATOS, HUNGARIAN ROMANI VIOLIN VIRUTOSO

LATIN STYLES

~ Calentano

~ Galician

~ Afro-Cuban

~ Tango

IT'S ALL ABOUT THE RHYTHM

There is a rich level of musicianship you can gain from exploring Latin string music because of the demanding rhythmic motifs. But the term "Latin" is misleading. It infers one culture, when in fact there are many Spanish-speaking countries, each with their own musical styles, instrumentation and repertoire. From the passionate Argentinian Tango, the smooth undulations of the Brazilian Bossa Nova, the fiery rhythms found in Afro-Cuban music, the orchestrated celebratory sounds of Mariachi and the indigenous violin style found in the Calentano style of Mexico, to the complex hybrid of musical ideas found in the Galician music of Spain, these styles couldn't be more different.

Rhythmically speaking, these styles do share a few attributes: syncopated phrases as well as surprising rhythmic twists and turns, the anticipation of the beat and the layering of rhythmic motifs. To master any of the styles in this book, you need to internalize the walking pulse that grounds each style, and, if you can't feel, hear and control entrances on the downbeats and upbeats in each measure, you will have tremendous difficulty playing true to each style. But most of the rhythmic ideas represented by the styles in this book are supported by the instrumentation associated with that style. So what's new here? It's the counter-rhythms played by the members of the ensemble. Most Latin styles create layers of rhythms within the group, so this would be like the difference between standing on one foot while leaning on a cane or crutch, versus standing on one foot while holding a bowling ball in one hand, a feather in the other, and wearing a lopsided hat on the side of your head.

Turn on a metronome at 60 and practice each of the following examples separately on quarter notes to get warmed up. Use a short down-bow to sound out the first and third beats, then switch to mark the second and fourth beats. Switch to an up-bow. Then repeat this exercise on the "and" of each beat. This requires hearing a steady eighth note pulse. There are two challenges here. The first is to accurately sound out your down and upbeats. The second is to use a short bow, thereby abbreviating the time value of each rhythm without rushing or cheating the steady 4/4 pulse:

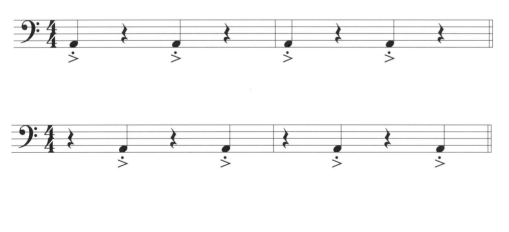

There are several ways to play a short, accentuated pitch. You can play at the frog with an elliptical shape to the motion of the bow to create a distinctive "drum-like hit" with each brief landing or you can leave the middle of the bow on the string and move it in the shape of a dash (—). Maintain a consistent volume from inception to silence. There are certainly more ways than this to abbreviate a pitch, but this is a good start. Any time you pay attention to sensation and sound through a new lens, you will increase technical mastery.

To play a syncopated rhythm requires hearing the sub-beats. For instance, if we use the 4/4 example on the previous page, you will need to hear and feel the eighth note pulse simultaneous to the walking quarter note, and even the sixteenth note pulse as a third layer. If you're in 6/8 time, the sixteenth note pulse layered over the eighth note walking pulse or, depending on the style, even smaller increments within the whole. To practice each of these examples, you might consider using your feet to walk the basic rhythm while you play each sub-rhythm. Use the backing track for help and make sure to apply small bows as a tool to maintain more precise control. You are laying foundation in preparation for what's to come.

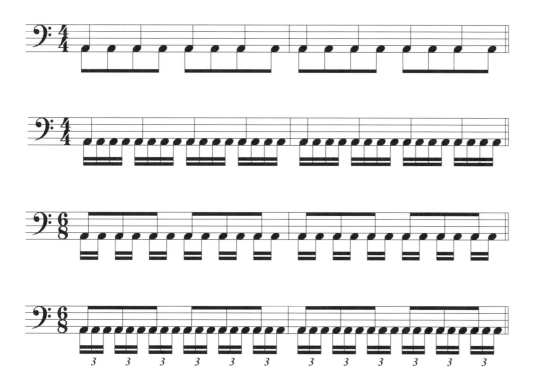

Now comes the tricky part. Hold onto these sounds in your ears as you play the examples on the following page. The idea isn't to solely play the written rhythm correctly, but to hear and feel the sub-rhythms that support it. By "feel," I don't mean bobbing your head or body or tapping your foot. It's less tangible than that, yet clear once mastered. Similar to dancing, the rhythms can be felt in the gut as if a drummer has set up residence in your torso.

When learning a new tune, always practice the rhythms separate from the pitches, then join them together. You can sing, clap, or walk the rhythms followed by playing them on an open string before adding in the left hand.

In the first example on the following page, I've provided two warm-ups to help you hear the sub-rhythmic foundation, followed by the actual rhythmic figure.

Now it's your turn to break down each of the following four rhythmic motifs into tangible practice steps:

Use the practice techniques we've covered as you delve into the tunes offered in the following pages.

CALENTANO

If it weren't for the years of archival work invested by fiddler Paul Anastasio, hardly anyone would know the Calentano style existed. When we think of Mexican music that includes bowed strings, "Mariachi" is on the tip of everyone's tongue. But Mariachi, while it uses violins, is not string-centric as is the case with Calentano music of Tierra Caliente. Mariachi has derived its material from the regional music of Mexico, but the violin parts are tightly arranged and the instrumentation for the band includes trumpets, a bass guitar called the *guitarron*, and a small guitar, the *vihuela*. Calentano is comprised of violin and guitar. As is the case with some of the styles we've covered thus far, once the violinist has performed the melody, he or she can tap into a large collection of ideas, called *adornos*, with which to create variations on the melody.

Unlike the music from Guadalajara, which over the years has grown from a regional style into the modern folk/pop hybrid now known as Mariachi, Calentano, the music of Tierra Caliente has languished in relative obscurity until quite recently.

The music of the Hot Lands grew from many of the same diverse musical roots as the many other Mexican regional styles. From Spain came the music of the bullfight ring, the dramatic pasodoble with its Moorish gapped scales. Europe contributed the waltz, scandalously romantic in its day; the march, with all its formality; and the cascading notes of the polka. Africa was the wellspring from which came stunning, often dizzyingly complex syncopation. The brilliant musicians of Cuba gave Tierra Caliente the bolero and danzón. Even the United States contributed to the mix, providing inspiration for the Hot Lands' own versions of foxtrots and swing tunes.

PAUL ANASTASIO, MULTI-STYLE FIDDLER AND WRITER

Originally a Norteño piece from northern Mexico, "El Huizache" was re-arranged in the gusto Calentano style many years ago by the Taviras, a family of fine musicians from Corral Falso, Guerrero. Violinist Juan Reynoso learned this piece from the Taviras, Paul Anastasio learned it from Juan Reynoso and I'm happy to share this tune with you, courtesy of Paul.

El Huizache

El Huizache (continued)

Juan Reynoso with Paul Anastasio

GALICIAN

When the dictator Francisco Franco died after ruling over Spain from 1939 to 1975, there was a cultural explosion of the traditional music of Galicia, a northwestern province of Spain. Franco advocated unity, and therefore suppressed Galician culture. After his death, this musical resurgence focused on the *gaita*, the Galician bagpipes, because unlike Irish music, which established the fiddle before the Uilleann Pipes, the gaita was the primary instrument that later influenced fiddling in Galicia.

When Klezmer fiddler and filmmaker Yale Strom made his movie, Carpati: 50 Miles, 50 Years (1996), he opened the film with a voiceover from Leonard Nimoy, saying, "I was born in Austro-Hungary, had my bris in Czechoslovakia, my bar mitzvah in Hungary, my wedding in the Soviet Union, and I'll be buried here in Ukraine and I never left my hometown."

This area of Spain reminds me of that opening line. From Roman to Germanic infiltration, as well as British Celts and the Moors—and these are just a few of the foreign influences—Spain represents a tremendous cultural melting pot. Yet throughout history, the original Galician culture struggled to maintain its own identity, still speaking and singing in Galician, a language that is related to Portuguese. Of note is the fact that Galicians are the only non-Castilian speaking people of Spain. The degree of Celtic influence on the music is disputed. Some claim the balance is 50/50 or more, while others think far less, if at all.

The violin was gradually integrated into traditional Galician music in the 1900s, mostly by a coterie of blind street violinists who earned their living playing and singing at fairs and in the marketplaces. I have included a few Galician tunes for you to enjoy, courtesy of the Galician bagpiper, Alexandre Cadarso.

To get started, make sure you can easily alternate between three-beat as well as two-beat figures over 6/8 time. This is a sub-rhythm used to accompany some Galician tunes.

Here are a few other rhythms you can practice to help familiarize yourself with the spicy feel of this style.

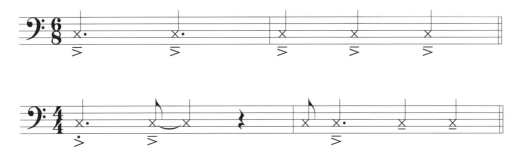

This first melody, "Xota de Fontaneira," was named after Fontaneira, a small village near Fonsagrada (Lugo), where the blind fiddler Florencio lived toward the end of his life. Notice how the third section modulates into a minor key. The structure of the tune is in three sections.

If we could travel in a time capsule back to when the two traditional Galician tunes included in this book were originally performed, we might have only heard solo fiddle. The few recordings I've been able to find for these tunes have been made fairly recently and it's impossible to determine whether or not they reflect traditional or contemporary arrangements of these tunes. Thus, the backing tracks will provide more of a rhythmic than harmonic accompaniment.

Xota de Fontaneira

TUNE DEMO

Each of the only three versions of this tune I've been able to find are in different keys, possibly because of how the melody for "Muiñeira de Cabana" sits on the bagpipes versus the fiddle. I have chosen to present it in two keys. The first version is thought to be the original key notated by the deceased composer, Manuel Figueroa Moreira, known also as "Manuel de O Bosque," from El Bosque—hence his nickname. He played the guitar, bandurria, clarinet, and bagpipes, and founded a group in the early 1900s.

Muiñeira de Cabana

in C harmonic minor

This second version was transcribed by Ricardo Santos Blanco, a member of the group Cántigas da Terra. When playing the tune, make sure to highlight the downbeat for the first of every three eighth notes as indicated:

Muiñeira de Cabana

in D harmonic minor

BACKING TRACK

AFRO-CUBAN

Starting in the 1500s, millions of Africans were captured by Spanish colonizers and transported to Brazil, Cuba, and America. This cruel practice, dubbed the "Atlantic Slave Trade," took place for four centuries. About 8,000 Africans, largely from West Africa, were transported to Cuba as slaves to work the sugar plantations. Most slaves managed to maintain their musical traditions as well as other aspects of their culture. Intermarriage gradually melded Latin and African cultures in Cuba as well as Brazil.

There is a strong history of violinists playing in Afro-Cuban ensembles, and as mentioned in the opening to this section of the book, the rhythmic challenges presented by this style will boost your playing skills.

A two-bar repeated pattern known as *clave* can be found at the heart of most Afro-Cuban music. The first pattern pictured below is referred to as a 2/3 pattern, the second, a 3/2 pattern.

The term, "Son," refers to a style developed in the Oriente province, now referred to as "son cubano." It's thought the original style incorporated the use of clave once rural musicians were exposed to the Havana-based "rumba" in the early 1900s. There are many other popular musical forms in Cuba, and a number of offshoots of son cubano, like "son montuno," "son oriental," "son santiaguero," and "son habanero"

> Son Cubano is defined by its vocal style, the use of syncopation, the incorporation of clave, parallel harmonies that run a third above the melody, and the instrumentation in the ensemble, which includes vocals, claves, bongo, maracas, güiro, double bass, trumpet, piano, and congas.

The tidal wave of interest in using a looper appears to be new. While the technology itself is fairly contemporary—though improvising cellist David Darling started using an early prototype called the Boomerang in the 1980s—the riff-oriented skill set required originates in African music. In particular, many styles throughout Africa include stacked layers of short melodic/rhythmic repetitious musical ideas.

The ability to build a series of rhythmic, melodic layers that integrate harmony and provide the supportive foundation for a melody requires a different approch to music than for Western canon. While classical music incorporates elements of repetition with a rhythmic underpinning, it is far more linear in construct. The complexity found in Afro-Cuban music can be attributed to the layering of contrasting rhythmic phrases built on top of the clave, whether salsa, bossa nova, samba, or Afro-Cuban.

Though there are two fundamental patterns, nowadays one can find many spin-off patterns as well. For instance, *son clave* offers its own 3/2 pattern and 2/3 pattern:

Familiarity with each of these rhythmic phrases will enable you to recognize and work with Latin rhythm sections, whether live or against a backing track. We will focus on an Afro-Cuban art form called *montuno*, a subgenre of son cubano. There are two popular chord patterns used in this art form. The first consists of I-V-V-I (one-five-five-one) harmonic pattern (C-G-G-C). If you don't feel comfortable practicing the double stops, first play the lower line, then the upper. This will give you a taste of the style and challenge you rhythmically.

"Montuno del Sol" is based on this second popular harmonic progression:

I-IV-V-IV

Consider practicing the root notes of the chords, followed by adding the third and fifth (C-E-G; F-A-C; and G-B-D) to familiarize yourself with the chord tones. After you play the melody, try to borrow rhythmic ideas from the clave and montuno examples as well as from "Montuno del Sol" to generate an improvisation over the backing track.

Montuno del Sol

by Julie Lyonn Lieberman

🔊 BACKING TRACK

The Afro-Cuban violin tradition is unusual in that it didn't emerge from an indigenous fiddle tradition but instead was created from the gradual marriage—over the course of nearly a century—of the European violin tradition with the rich and complex

traditions of West and Central African drumming. The charanga ensemble, with flute, two violins (and sometimes cello), piano, bass, timbales, conga, and guiro gradually developed over time from its role playing danzones for upper crust dances to being in the forefront of nearly every important Cuban popular music style of the 20th century including cha-cha, mambo and songo.

The violin plays several roles in the charanga ensemble. The most important of these is as a vital member of the rhythm section, locking in with the drums, hearing simultaneous interlocking parts, and phrasing the montuno patterns in such a way that keep the dancers moving. Violinists are also called on to take improvised solos. Musicians such as El Niño Prodigio, Pupi Legarreta, Jose "Chombo" Silva and Alfredo de la Fe developed an innovative improvisational language that showcases the unique history and aesthetic of Afro-Cuban music.

SAM BARDFELD, MULTI-STYLE VIOLINIST AND AUTHOR OF "LATIN VIOLIN"

TANGO

Let's travel to Argentina, home of the tango. As you may have gleaned by now, any location that has a port and therefore hosts a number of cultures provides just the right recipe for an interesting new style of music. In this case, by the 1920s, Argentina's bustling city, Buenos Aires, had become home to the Italians, Spanish, French, Africans, and British.

The dance form known as *milongo* was popular among Afro-Argentine club-goers in the late 1800s. A partner dance, it featured elaborate footwork between the man and woman. Then, *canbombe*, an African slave dance, infused this dance style with freely improvised steps, wild rhythms, and improvisation between the dancers. The dance style and the music invited a fusion of the emotional with the physical and the musicians—on guitar, flute, harp and violin—would improvise to accompany them. It's a passionate art form and the 1910s introduction of the German bellows-driven instrument, the *bandoneon*, made a substantial contribution to the sound we currently recognize as *tango*.

Today, musicians perceive tango as a carefully composed style of music. That's because of composer Astor Piazolla's brilliant contributions to the art form, called *nuevo tango*. International acclaim established his compositions as the gold standard worldwide, and improvisation, while still present in the dance form, was replaced by tightly composed pieces.

This style is a fantastic doorway for classically trained string players into a new style. That's because, unlike many or most of the styles covered in this book, the genre invites full-blown vibrato, lush, sweeping bows and technical prowess.

Here is a signature rhythm that underpins many tango compositions:

Tango is characterized by two main rhythms:

There are two typical harmonic progressions used in tango music, but you can find a number of variations as well. The lower case means minor and the 7 indicates a flatted seventh:

i - i - V7 - V7 - V7 - V7 - i - i

i - iv - V7 - i - i - iv - DVI - V7

Fiddling the Tango

by Julie Lyonn Lieberman

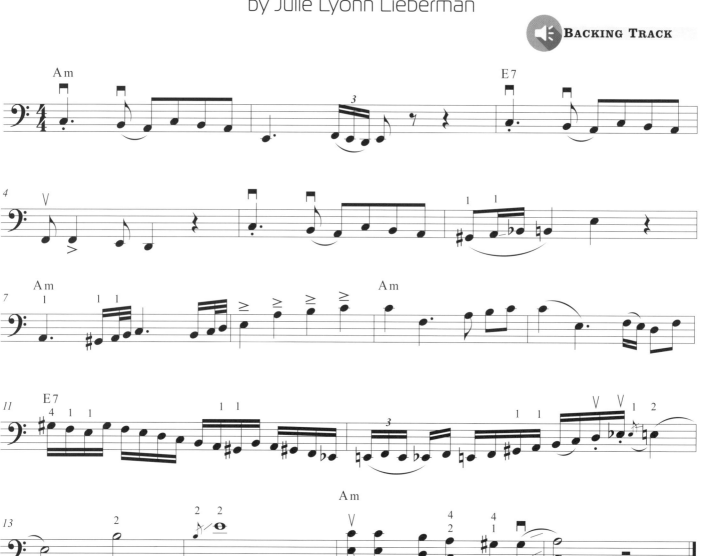

When performing in a tango style we've got to keep in mind its origins: tango is a dance form reliant on a very stable and metronomic rhythmic drive. In the 1990s I worked with a group of twelve tangueros from Buenos Aires in a show called "Forever Tango." One comment I heard while training with them really stuck with me and eventually found its way into my tango playing: "Think of this as being in 1/4 as opposed to 4/4." In other words, each beat in the bar carries the same gravity as the downbeat, so stay with the quarter note pulse and don't accentuate the downbeats only. This structural style of playing results in a melodic line that carries a strong sense of improvised freedom when juxtaposed over and around a strict percussive underpinning. When playing rhythmic tango lines, think of yourself as a percussionist as well as a melodic player. Real tango emerges when the melodies soar above this rock solid structure.

JEREMY COHEN, MULTI-GENRE VIOLINIST AND COMPOSER

A COLLAGE OF STYLES

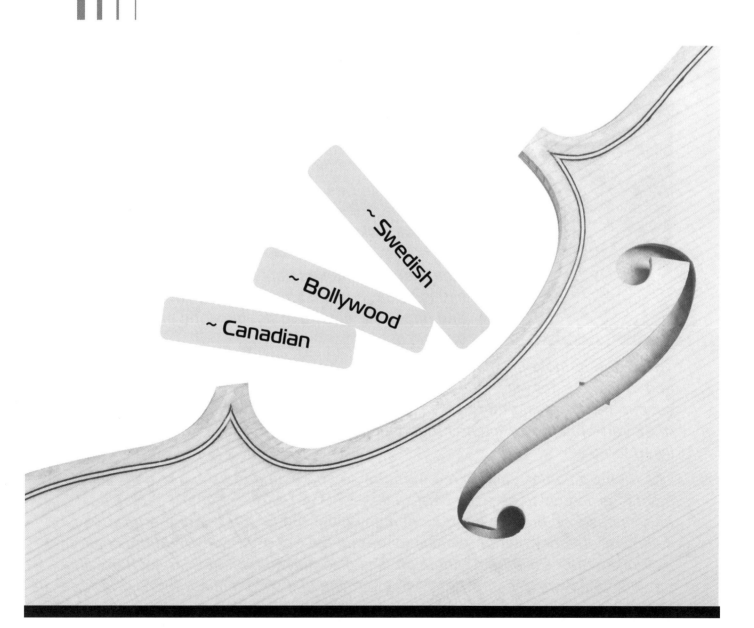

~ Swedish

~ Bollywood

~ Canadian

SWEDISH

I learned my first group of Swedish fiddle tunes when Jay Ungar hired me to play in the early 1980s for actress Liv Ullman's birthday. Alongside Jay and players like Matt Glaser and Evan Stover, I'm quite sure our fiddle styling was no more correct than our costumes!

Fiddling is prevalent throughout the Nordic countries, but more so in Sweden and Norway than in Denmark, Finland, and Iceland. Fiddle is central to Swedish folk music, as is, in some parts of Sweden, the *nyckelharpa*, a bowed stringed instrument worn with a strap around the neck and positioned fairly similarly to that of a guitar. It is tuned like a viola—A, D, G and a drone C—with twelve additional strings that ring in sympathy and aren't bowed. The highly decorated Norwegian fiddle is called a *hardingfele* or *Hardanger* fiddle and is outfitted with four bowed and four or five sympathetic strings.

The traditional tunes, beginning in the 1600s and possibly earlier, were mainly designed to accompany dance, and the most popular form is the *polska*. Tunes are played solo and in a twin fiddle setting, as well as in larger ensembles. Polskas are Sweden's national dance and can be eighth-note, sixteenth-note or triplet based, but always in 3/4 time. There are more contemporary dances from the 1900s, *gammaldans*, that employ 3/4 and 2/4 meter.

Swedish traditional music is emotionally rich—deep, blissful, melancholy, joyous—and very easy to fall in love with! It's often played as an intimate duo with the harmony player improvising a parallel part.

Being a fiddle-based tradition, it's all about the bow. Each regional polska dance variant requires a particular svikt (gradient of ups and downs) which the bow conveys. Some have a powerful tidal surge while others are like horses cantering over low hills or birds flitting through long summer nights. Trills, both over and under the note, and doublestops are found in varying degrees.

The sixteenth note polskas are generally even in rhythm, while the eighth note and to some extent the triplet polskas can be internally crooked, e.g. a longer second beat and shorter third, which can lead the ear to guess they're in seven or eleven—but the dance and the tune flow together as a not-quite-metronomic, living three.

The tunes Julie has chosen are from the southern slängpolska tradition. They have a strong pulse on each beat, with a rocking heartbeat quality, and also an emphasis on the first beat. As in many older tunes, there are quarter-tones, called vallåtstoner (herding-music tones) on the 3rd, 6th, and 7th of the scale. In "Polska efter Pelle Fors," the high G is also played a bit high. In modernizing these sounds, we get surprising and charming shifts from minor to major and back.

ANDREA HOAG, SWEDISH AND AMERICAN FIDDLER

Polska efter Pelle Fors

Svanpolskan efter Pelle Fors

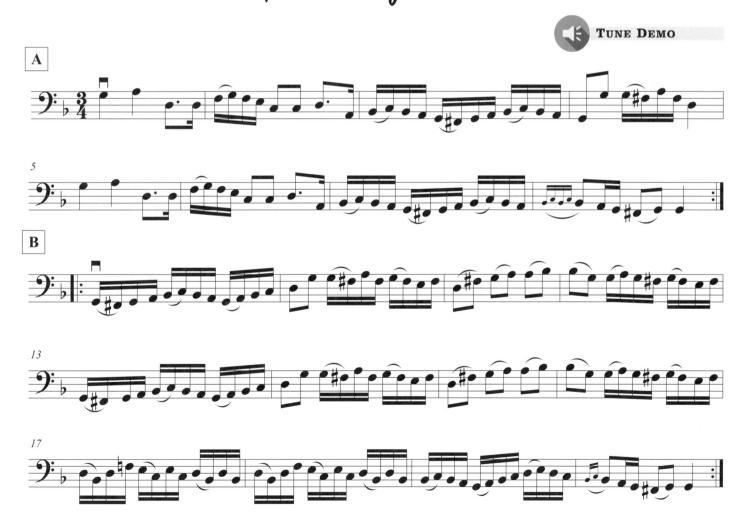

EAST INDIAN

Two styles of music exist in India: Carnatic of the South and Hindustani of the North. There are shared as well as divergent characteristics between the two styles.

The classical training system is far more extensive than any I've encountered. Students spend long days at their teacher's home. They learn alongside the music guru's other students in private and group sessions and even help out with household chores. The rhythms and scales are learned vocally against a drone first for at least five years before the individual touches his or her chosen instrument. This is true for percussion (Tabla, Mridangam and Dholak to name a few) as well as for melodic instruments.

In contrast to the West, where we have a handful of functional (in every-day use) rhythms, like 4/4, 2/4, 6/8 and 3/4, Indian music is made up of over one hundred functional rhythms (*tala*), including 13/8 and even 17½/8! The same can be said about scales. The West offers major and minor as well as the seven modes and jazz chordal scales applied when soloing in jazz. Indian music is based on roughly three-hundred ragas, and the *aaroh* (ascent) and *avroh* (descent) of a scale may be different.

The Hindustani *raga* is a springboard for improvisation in the North after the melody is performed, whereas Carnatic musicians focus on the ornamentation of the *kriti* (melody). The musician tracks rhythmic patterns within the architecture of the tala and some of these rhythmic latticeworks are quite lengthy.

Bollywood is India's Hollywood version of their traditional music. "River of Bollywood" has been designed to give you a small taste of some of the sounds from this region of the world.

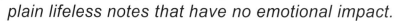

Indian music comes from an aural tradition which is passed on from teacher to student without using sheet music. Learning the phrases of a raga by ear becomes internalized, and later with practice, reproduced. It's primarily the vocal tradition that uses gamak (ornaments) widely. Without gamak, there are only plain lifeless notes that have no emotional impact.

The timing of a phrase is about the length of a singer's breath. That translates to a long bow in Gayaki Ang, a vocal style of violin playing. It's complex to perform the specifics because these are timed, accurate, micro movements of the left hand without using the western violin technique of shifting. Shifting is not a fluid enough technique to accommodate this music. Gamak technique explores the space, the timing of and connections between chosen pitches. Some call this sliding or gliding which is too simple because it has specific timing and direction.

Each raga has characteristic defining phrases. The duration of notes, and the carefully woven approach to the notes in a phrase, are part of the greater overarching development when revealing the subtleties of a raga.

VICKI RICHARDS, WEST MEETS EAST VIOLINIST

River of Bollywood

by Julie Lyonn Lieberman

CANADIAN FIDDLE STYLES

 A number of fiddle styles can be found in Canada. Earlier in the book, we discussed the Scottish-inspired Cape Breton style, but there are also the Métis and Québécois styles and a vast well of fiddle repertoire from each region of Canada, like Prince Edward Island and New Brunswick. Canadian fiddle tunes generally consist of varying blends of Scottish, Irish, and French repertoire and techniques. Many tunes are organized symmetrically, AABB, and squared off into eight-bar phrases, but there are also a number of tunes that don't follow this simple, predictable pattern. They are called *crooked tunes*.

Of particular note are players like Don Messer from New Brunswick, Andy DeJarlis of the Métis style, April Verch, Buddy MacMaster, Jerry Holland, Natalie MacMaster, and Donnell Leahy. Traditional fiddler, educator, and composer Calvin Vollrath who's inspired many Canadian fiddlers and to date, has composed hundreds of fiddle tunes.

When my father, fiddler Art "Lefty" Vollrath, was a teenager, he was exposed to the Métis style of fiddling. The tunes are crooked and tough to figure out. I grew up listening to him play in this style, among others, and was also influenced by French, Scottish, and Scandinavian tunes.

My father told me before I played my first dance at age fifteen, "You find the best dancers on the floor, like barley floating in the wind, and you follow one couple. They'll set your tempo all night long." The dances that used to be plentiful in the 1960s, 70s, and 80s are less now, but whenever I play, I'm thinking dance. And I'm imagining that I hear the square dance callers because their rhythm was so bang on as they called the dances. The fiddler had to put lots of drive in the bow. The notes were important, but the feel was everything.

There was a Métis fiddler named Lee Creemo who once said to me, "The fiddle is the voice and the bow is the tongue." When I teach, I try to get students to accept that they don't have to play exactly like me. I'm going to play differently every day because I play with passion. I tell them, "Play from your heart. I will teach you the notes, but you have to make those notes dance. It's you who has to create music out of those notes. Don't copy. Play from your heart. Make music."

CALVIN VOLLRATH, CANADIAN FIDDLER AND COMPOSER

The Métis trace their descent to intermarriage between French fur traders and a healthy sprinkling of English and Scots, with two indigenous peoples of Canada, the Cree and Saulteaux. The fiddle, played by Scottish immigrants as well as French fur traders, became a wonderful voice with which to express the music of the fusion of these diverse cultures. There are a number of versions of "Red River Jig" in varying meter and the tune is often referred to as the Métis national anthem. The Red River runs through Maritoba, an important territory for the Métis. The tune is actually a reel, not a jig. Notice how it starts high and then drops to the lower pitches in the B section.

Red River Jig

"Levis Beaulieu" is one of my favorite Québécois tunes. The B section offers a wonderful interplay between A major and A mixolydian with its flatted seventh. You can add drones against the A and E in the B section if so desired. I've seen this tune referred to as "Beaulieu Reel," but there is an entirely different melody referred to by that same name as well.

Levis Beaulieu

Every style we've covered in *A Festival of Violin & Fiddle Styles* deserves its own book, and those are just the string-centric styles. Nowadays, string players can incorporate any style they're attracted to into their vocabulary, whether or not that style is string-centric.

Thank you for joining the exploration!

Books, DVDs & String Orchestra Scores by Julie Lyonn Lieberman

Books

Rockin' Out with Blues Fiddle (HL00695612)

Improvising Violin (HL00695234)

The Contemporary Violinist (HL00695420)

You Are Your Instrument: The Definitive Musician's Guide to Practice and Performance (HL00695233)

The Creative Band and Orchestra (HL00842063)

How to Play Contemporary Strings (HL00151529)

Twelve-Key Practice: The Path to Mastery and Individuality (HL00286780)

A Festival of Violin & Fiddle Styles (HL00298177)

DVDs

Rhythmizing the Bow (HL00320461)

Techniques for the Contemporary String Player (HL00320498)

The Violin in Motion (HL00320533)

Violin and Viola Ergonomics (HL00320986)

Vocal Aerobics (HL00320723)

Multi-Genre String Orchestra Scores

Alfred Music:

Midnight's Celtic Run (Celtic), *Folk Dance From Provence* (Provencal), *Rockin' It* (rock), *Lebedike Honga* (Klezmer), *Hotter Than Blues* (Blues), *Twin Sisters* (Old-time with a Celtic twinge), *Flop Eared Mule* (Old-time), *Blues Fiddle on the Fringe* (blues), *Terkisher Klezmer Celebration* (Klezmer), and *Mason's Apron* (Celtic).

Kendor Music:

French Roast (Provencal), *A Cinematic Journey* (pop), *Celtic Butterfly* (Irish), *Klezmer Fest* (Klezmer), *Bollywood Strings* (East Indian), and *TechnoStrings* (rock).